*La Duchesse de Langeais
and Other Plays*

La Duchesse de Langeais
and Other Plays

Michel Tremblay

translated by John Van Burek

Talonbooks   •   Vancouver   •   1976

published with assistance from the Canada Council

Talonbooks
201 1019 East Cordova
Vancouver
British Columbia V6A 1M8
Canada

This book was typeset by Linda Gilbert of B.C. Monthly
Typesetting Service, and printed in Canada by Hignell Printing Ltd.

Second printing: February 1993

"La Duchesse de Langeais" first published with *Hosanna* by Les
Editions Leméac Inc., Montréal, Québec. "Berthe," "Johnny
Mangano and His Astonishing Dogs" and "Gloria Star" first
published as *Trois Petits Tours* by Les Editions Leméac Inc., Montréal,
Québec.

Canadian Shared Cataloguing in Publication Data

Tremblay, Michel, 1942–
    La duchesse de Langeais & other plays

    ISBN 0-88922-104-9

    I. Title.
    PS8539.R47D8313   C842'.5'4   C77-002031-3
    PQ3919.2.T73D8313

"La Duchesse de Langeais" was first performed by Les Insolents de Val d'Or in Val d'Or, Québec, in the spring of 1969, with the following cast:

La Duchesse   Doris Saint-Pierre

Directed by Hélène Bélanger

"La Duchesse de Langeais" was also performed at Théâtre de Quat' Sous in Montréal, Québec, in March, 1970, with the following cast:

La Duchesse   Claude Gai

Directed by André Brassard

"Berthe," "Johnny Mangano and His Astonishing Dogs" and "Gloria Star" were first performed as "Trois Petits Tours" on French language CBC-TV in the series, "Beaux Dimanches," on December 21, 1969, with the following casts:

"Berthe"

Berthe   Denise Proulx

"Johnny Managano and His Astonishing Dogs"

Carlotta	Denise Filiatrault
Johnny Mangano	Jacques Godin
M.C.	Jacques Bilodeau
Stage Manager	Dominique Briand

"Gloria Star"

Margot	Sophie Clément
Laurette	Luce Guilbeault
Diane	Claudette Delorimier
Gigi	Yolande Michot
Lise	Marie-Claire Nolin
The Woman	Denise Pelletier
Stage Manager	Dominique Briand

Paul	Ernest Guimond
M.C.	Jacques Bilodeau

Directed by Paul Blouin

"Surprise, Surprise" was first performed by Théâtre-Midi du Maurier at the Théâtre du Nouveau Monde in Montréal, Québec, in April, 1975, with the following cast:

Jeannine	Monique Joly
Laurette	Denise Morelle
Madeleine	Carmen Tremblay

Directed by André Brassard

"Surprise, Surprise" was first performed in English at the St. Lawrence Centre in Toronto, Ontario, on October 30, 1975, with the following cast:

Jeannine	Marilyn Lightstone
Laurette	Jayne Eastwood
Madeleine	Brenda Donahue

Directed by Eric Steiner

La Duchesse de Langeais

Act One

*A "terrasse de café." "La Duchesse de Langeais,"
an aging queen about sixty years old, vacationing
somewhere in the sunny climes, is seated in front
of a half-empty bottle of scotch. She is already
visibly under the weather.*

*The character, "la Duchesse de Langeais,"
should be as effeminate as possible. No wiggle
of the hips, wave of the hand or "wink perverse"
should be spared. The caricature should be
complete, perfect . . . and touching. "La Duchesse" often tries to speak à la française, but
her "joual" origins always show through.*

*She is wearing dreadful American summer
clothes: powder blue "chino" trousers, a three-
buttoned shirt of the same colour and white
straw shoes.*

As the lights come up, "la Duchesse" is resting her head in her left hand, her elbow on the table. With her right hand she is toying with her empty glass. She seems very much distracted.

After a moment, she smiles sadly and pours herself a hefty drink. With dignity, she stands and walks downstage, her hand raised as if in a toast.

LA DUCHESSE:
Tonight, we don't make love, we get drunk!

She empties her glass in one shot.

That's right, girls! Fini, l'amour, fini, fini! The final strains and then no more!

She staggers a little.

Jesus, that's strong! Garçon!

Very woman of the world.

Garçon, what have you put in this drink? It's dreadful! Oh, silly me. The garçon has gone for his "siesta." There are no garçons at this time of day . . .

She sighs.

You're all alone, little girl . . . No wonder, hein? Who else but you would sit on the terrasse in heat like this? Hélas, a woman of the world is a woman of the world. One must maintain one's "standing." What's more, sonny boy, I just woke up, so I'm hardly gonna take a nap now! Barbarous custom! God, are you stupid! A real screwball!

She laughs.

8

You're the honest to goodness queen of the Nellies.
Good thing I know it, hein? . . . Oh, as for knowing
that, do I ever know that! No one can tell me I don't
know that. For forty years I've been telling the whole
world!

She plants herself full front à la Marlene Dietrich.

That's right, Your Honour, forty years of service with
the very best of references. A la française, à la grecque,
tout ce que vous voulez. And première class!

With a big dramatic laugh.

I am a praying mantis, a devourer of males.

Another big dramatic laugh.

When they talk about me, they always say, "la Duchesse? A raving queen! The biggest faggot that ever
came down the pike!" But you think I give a shit?
I know it's true! Doesn't bother me. Not in the least.
And the ones who say it are no better anyway. They're
powdered up, queen-faced faggots just like me. That's
all. Oh, they can all go . . .

She pauses.

I'm thirsty . . .

*She struts back to the table, wiggling her bum,
and pours herself a drink.*

No more ice. You mean I have to drink it straight?
Yech, sick to my stomach. Oh, what the hell, you
can do it! Bottoms up, ma chérie. Give the monsieur a
glimpse of your talents . . .

*She drinks it down in one shot, then howls like
a circus barker.*

Ta-raaam! Et voilà! La Duchesse has just consumed a disgusting glass of disgusting booze in one unfaltering swig POUR-LE-MONSIEUR! Ta-daaam!

She falls onto her chair under the effect of the alcohol.

Ouais! . . . Well, my pixie, you're really outdoing yourself.

She throws her head back.

That sun is like Chinese torture! . . . That's alright, it's good for you. You'll be all tanned and beautiful.

She wipes her face.

That's not true, Cinderella, 'cause all you ever do in the sun is turn red as a lobster. Oh, a lobster! Mon Dieu! That's masculin! Am I gonna start referring to myself in the masculin! Quelle horreur! Of course, there must be lady lobsters, but still . . . Oh, go on, have another drink, chérie, then we'll go cruise for a bit, see if we can't scare up some game in the under-brush . . . Ouais ben, don't waste your time, dear. The beaches are empty at this hour . . . The god-damned "siesta!" I am sick of the "siesta!" . . . Ah, the men must all be sleeping now, their tails gently resting . . . "Softly draped upon the thigh," as I would say if I were a poétesse . . .

She sings:

"La poésie fout le camp, François Villon!" Of course with me, poetry hasn't descended into the streets. It's descended into the shit! "La poésie fout le camp . . ."

She stops suddenly.

That reminds me . . . Mon Dieu! It's been ages since I've thought about him.

She laughs.

Aie, you really gotta be plastered to have him come back to mind, the little worm . . . Well, well, well, this calls for another drink!

Same routine as at the beginning.

Tonight we don't make love, we get drunk!

She drinks.

Goodness me, my poet . . . That goes back a long, long time. I'd forgotten all about him . . .

Very woman of the world.

Tucked away in my memory, like a precious jewel . . .

With a great dramatic sigh.

The silly twit! What a number! I guess he finally did manage to publish a few poems . . . That's right too, I remember now . . . On the circuit they used to call him "Bite my shoulder" because of a poem he once wrote for me . . . Can you believe it? "Bite my shoulder!" . . . And he made love like a herd of cattle. Hopeless . . .

Coughing mixed with laughter.

Be careful, Alice . . . Let me see, I met him . . . that was before Sandra's club . . . I think I found him on the street . . . A good girl, as usual . . . right in front of the "Cinéma de Paris" where la Vaillancourt was taking tickets . . . He used to play at being the poor suffering poet and while la Vaillancourt would tear your ticket, he'd tear your heart out! Hah! All he

needed was a pair of big ears and he's have made
a perfect Gérard Philippe . . . Oh, what was his name?
. . . Don't dig too deeply, hein, you'll get me all
excited . . .

She laughs.

At your age! Tsk, tsk, tsk! You're so pretentious!

A wink, a little squeal and a wiggle of the hips.

I called him, "my lover with the brazen shaft." I
don't know why. Guess I thought it sounded nice.
God knows, that's the only thing about him that was
the least bit hard . . . And I was stuck with the little
pisspot for two whole months . . . He couldn't do
a thing! Nothing! Had to show him everything! Toute!
From beginning to end! Mon Dieu, the crazy things
I've done in my life. No one in Montréal has had
more "aventures stupides" than me. I could tell you
about them for weeks, my darlings. Why, in the last
forty years, there's been no one in the whole of
Montréal who's known more people than me, and
who's balled more people than me. I've spent my life
at it, girls, I've spent my life at it. Never anything
else . . . Fucking, fucking, fucking . . . Darling, you're
so vulgar! If the vacationing CBC girls ever heard you!
It's a good thing they're taking their "siestas," hein?
Why, the poor dears, they'd swoon on the spot if
they heard you talk like that! Because, can you believe
it, nowadays when they meet me, they're ashamed!

Very woman of the world.

Eh, oui! That's what they told me, like this, with their
lips all pinched and their pinkies in the air . . . They
want nothing more to do with me if I don't clean up
my act. "You call yourself 'Duchesse,' you should set
a good example." Aie, wow, hein? Nothing but . . .
snotty ladies! Bloody bitches! I'd scratch their faces if
I still had my nails! They make me sick, lying around

on the beach, playing Madame . . . Like they were queens of the world . . . They've got about as much class as . . . And of course, they haven't got two cents to rub together! Oh, I know them all, those CBC whores who come down here on vacation. Queers, tapettes, every one of them! Cocksuckers, all of them! The whole bloody gang! There are a few who try to be males, but they just look like constipated whores. It's a long time since I've been fooled, hein? I can smell a queer a hundred miles away! That means I've always got a nose full, but that's another story . . . Yesterday, my dear ladies, they were eating les fruits de mer, sprawled all over the beach, pinkies in the air, yeah, in the air, and they'd coo with pleasure and roll back their eyes everytime they'd pop a little fishie into their mouths . . . But back in Montréal, they'd die of fright if they saw a fly in their soup. Aie, wow, hein? I mean there's ridiculous and ridiculous! No, that doesn't work with me anymore. I wasn't born yesterday and these "princesses" from Montréal, Canada haven't impressed me for a long time. Look, I've got forty years experience and a few thousand men up my ass, so I can afford to play "la Duchesse" . . . But them, they're not even thirty years old and they want to play woman of the world. Between you and me, hein? . . . All they manage to look like is cheap little Jewish ladies coming out of the five and dime . . . Their petits bleached hairdos, their petits fingernails all filed, their petits bikinis transparent and their cute little petit walk . . . that they copied from me . . . Aie, wow, hein? Grow up a little first, sister, then come see your aunt. You can play the ingénue all you want, but not la femme du monde! If it's lessons you want, I'll give them to you, free of charge, but don't try to pass for a pro. Not in front of me! . . . Tiens, my glass is empty. God, the way this stuff disappears! Maybe there are ghosts, eh?

Very woman of the world.

13

I'm also very well read, you know? Garçon, un autre drink.

She starts to pour herself another drink.

Keep this up and the poor dears will find you under the table when they wake up from their naps . . .

Again, the same routine as at the beginning of the play.

Tonight, we don't make love . . .

She stops suddenly.

Love! Fuck! I'd almost fogotten it!

She runs to get the bottle and comes back downstage.

Tonight we get drunk! Paquetée! Blotto!

She drinks. A long silence.

LA DUCHESSE paces about like a lion in a cage.

You think I'm gonna start bawling like a fat Italian, throw myself on the ground and tear out the last three hairs on my head, hein? Well, you're sadly mistaken! You won't see me cry. The way I feel right now . . . Take a good look, hein? . . . The way I feel right now, I am unhappy like I've never been unhappy in my life! And you know why? That's right, my little lambies, you've guessed it . . . Love.

She climbs onto a chair and lifts her arms in the air.

"La Duchesse de Langeais" has a broken heart.

Silence.

Tell it to the firemen, they'll piss all over you! La Duchesse, heartbroken? Impossible! After forty years in the business? Yeah, me too, that's what I always thought, that after forty years, you had no more heart. Well, get a load of this, my little pixies. When, after forty years experience, you realize that you still do have a heart . . . Stop it, Alice, stop it! That's sentimental shit. Don't tell me you're going to get shitty. A woman of the world never gets shitty in public. A woman of the world shits on the public! I shit on the whole world.

She drinks, choking a little.

Amen.

She gets down off the chair.

I'm as drunk as a baby after its suck! If only I could have a good burp and go to sleep. Sleeping Beauty.

In a neutral tone, without conviction.

Last year I went to a costume party at la Choquette's dressed as Sleeping Beauty. I never saw people laugh so hard.

She sits down. Silence.

Crazy old "Duchesse," I love you anyway . . . You're the most beautiful, and the most loveable . . .

She gets up suddenly, her arms in the air.

Aren't I beautiful? Maybe not any longer, but I used to be. Oui, monsieur! I was stunning! I had the whole of Montréal at my feet. I won't tell you what year that was, but it's true all the same. All of Montréal, at my feet! When I started doing la Duchesse, they came from miles to see me! All the men, the real ones, the males, the bulls, would crawl before me in the hopes that I would deign to look at them. I'd push them, like this, with the tip of my foot . . . That was in the days when I was a star . . . I was a grande artiste in my own genre . . . Even today, when I put myself to it, I can make a small crowd drool over me! I've still got a few tricks to turn that aren't all worm-eaten . . . A woman of experience is a woman of experience, hein? I mean, a slut like me, even if she's a duchesse, has to be able to rise to every occasion. Men are very demanding, you never know what they're going to ask of you. That's why I've always kept a "répertoire." A répertoire of star performances . . . Look, when you're good enough to make a man think that he's sleeping with a famous international star, but that his international star is really just a man, because it's with a man that he really wants to go to bed, well, hat's off to Mary! And those of you who've got hats, you can take them off to me, okay? Yeah, I know, nowadays it's Sophie Tucker, Tallulah Bankhead and Josephine Baker, but in the old days, dans ma jeunesse . . .

Very "actrice."

You should have seen me doing Edwidge Feuillère in the final scene from "La Dame aux Camélias!"

She throws her head way back and coughs a little.

I was sublime! I used to do that for my ice salesman . . . He wept buckets, the poor dear, enough to tear your heart out! Then he'd hand me twenty-five bucks! For my roller-skating dancer, it was Esther Williams. You should have seen me in a bathing suit! A real siren! And not one that finished in the tail of a mermaid, believe me! The towel around the head, the whole bit! I'd sing, "Take Me Out to the Ball Game," and the walls would come tumbling down! Oh, they tumbled, alright, from the ecstatic blows of my swooning lover . . . For my actors . . . 'cause

I had countless actors, countless . . . I had two numbers that were showstoppers like you've never seen! Listen to this . . . The first was Marguerite Jamois in "Britannicus." Wow! She was "Agripping" all over the place, okay? Nails this long, the jaw way out front, the bust at nose level, nostrils flaring . . . I was spectaculaire! "It was during the horror of a pitch black night . . ." No, wait . . . That's from "Phaedre!" Anyway . . . The second number . . . Now get a load of this . . . This was my masterpiece . . . Sarah Bernhardt en personne playing "Hamlet!" Complete with the wooden leg! Is that good enough for you? I even had one of those little soldier costumes . . . It was incredible. I almost looked like a man. And the quotes, I'd spout off speeches one after another. And if it had been the style, I'd have had posters printed too . . . Of course, I had a raft of other imitations for my less important lovers . . . Pauline Carton reciting Sacha Guitry . . . It wasn't sexy-sexy, but it did the trick . . . Bette Davis in "The Letter!" I'd get my eyes big as saucers and I'd walk all crooked . . . Barbara Stanwyck, Arletty, Mae West . . . "Come up and see me sometime, sucker!" When I felt like a real queen, I'd do my Shirley Temple. The frizzy wig, the whole bit. I've even done Galina Oulanova dancing "Swan Lake!"

She crouches, more or less, into the dying swan position from "Swan Lake."

By the time I quit, I had it down to a "t." I mean, I could die like no ballerina has ever died before . . . Have you ever seen me doing Claudette Colbert in "Cleopatra" where I take my milk bath? Seventy-eight bucks worth of milk in my tub! And in those days, seventy-eight bucks, hein? . . . As the old whores say, "Those were the days . . ."And I used to do cabaret too . . . back in the Fifties . . .

Laughing.

What if I told you that Mac Orlan wrote a number for me?

She goes toward the table, pours what's left of the scotch into her glass and drinks it down in one shot.

Get a load of this . . . Maestro, musique, s'il vous plaît . . .

She sings the first stanza of "La Chanson de Margaret" by Pierre Mac Orland.

The streets of le Havre were my only classmates,
With the whores of the port in old Chloé's bar.
In an alley in Tampico the cold hand of fate
Took hold of my life and said "follow this star."
Now it's easy to say that money don't smell,
But the oil down there will prove it's a lie.
And down Tampico way, when your luck goes to hell,
You past will come back to spit in your eye.
So that's where I left my innocence behind,
Deflowered forever in old Tampico.
A sweet, blushing babe with only one thing in mind,
To sell what I had and bring in the dough.
With a smile and a hustle I made lots of deals,
I peddled my wares and kept paying my dues.
In a dump like that, who cares what you feel,
Even the marijuana gives you the blues.

When she finishes her song, she sits down.

Yep, even Mac Orlan knew about me . . . 'Cause Tampico, hein, I was there . . . For six months I was assistant striptease at some club in the red light district . . . I caught the clothes when the broad tossed them off.

Dreamily.

Of course, all that was before I became la Duchesse. I wasn't yet a woman of the world . . . But, you know, that's where I met my first real sugar daddy . . . A German playboy with looks like a god. He'd never slept with a man before, but once he'd been cuddled in lovergirl's arms, he turned tail, like that! It was him who introduced me to the world . . . It was him who taught me the first rudiments of my future career as duchesse, as it were. And it was him who took me on my first trip to Europe! Eh, oui! Europe! Before that I didn't believe it really even existed. But then, after three or four countries, I got bored with my German god. I did the rest of the tour "freelance." When I came back to Montréal, I was walking on clouds. A woman of the world in every wonderful sense of the term! I started giving "teas" for my lady friends every Sunday afternoon . . . La Choquette, la Dubeau, la Rolande Saint-Germain . . . What a queen she was! . . . la Steeman, la Rochon, all the royalty of Montréal was there . . . Every Sunday afternoon they'd arrive at my place, all girdled up and dressed to the nines, floor-length gowns, high heels, you name it . . . La Rochon would show up wearing her mink stole, even in the middle of August . . . We'd sit there, stiff as boards, and sip tea with our pinkies in the air. After that, we'd play chamber music! La Rochon played the flute, la Steeman, the violin, la Rolande Saint-Germain, crazy as ever, would play the French horn . . . We called her "le fond du cor au son des bois" . . . La Dubeau, the mandolin, and me, your humble servant, played the piano . . . You should have heard the music! Unbelievable! A ladies orchestra the likes of which the world had never seen before, nor has it ever since! And it was a no nonsense affair, hein? We meant business! If anyone started acting up, she'd hear about it for the rest of the afternoon. We lasted quite a while with that . . . Two years, I think . . . Once we even played in a charity show . . . We called ourselves "The Ladies Morning Club, Junior." An unprecedented success! The men clapped so hard,

they got blisters on their hands! I know, 'cause that's
the time I spent the night with the husband of my
sister, Pauline, who was in the hospital . . .

She shrugs her shoulders and laughs.

You know, it's awful when I think about the things
I have done in my life . . . I've almost gone around
the world . . . On my ass! Richer than Cresus or poor
as Orphan Annie . . . With a life like that you never
know what you'll find between your legs . . . And
I worked like a slave too, to get where I am today.
Mind you, I don't regret a thing, hein? Not a thing!
Whatever I did, I did it because I wanted to. I wasn't
interested in spending my life as a two-bit queer in
Montréal, Canada. Not me! My ambitions were of a
larger scope . . . For starters, international whore.
After that, Duchesse! You know, I've been laid on
four continents! America, Europe, Asia and Africa.
I never made it to Australia . . . Oui, quatre continents! I've seen all colours and all sizes, if you know
what I mean . . . But it's because I like it that way.
I chose my profession! And I've had one beautiful
life! Okay, so nowadays I usually pay for a screw,
but it's only lately that I've started doing that. Furs,
jewels, limousines, la Duchesse has had them all!
Aie, when I got taken out, it wasn't to go to some
chintzy movie, hein? Oh no, her highness always
chose the most expensive and the most exquisite.
And not many people dared to refuse, because her
anger was infamous and they knew what would
happen if they ever said "No." And it was like that
for years! For years!

Silence.

That's right, mes chéries, la Duchesse is a somebody!
And she has nothing to regret. Well, almost . . . Just
this goddamned little business . . . Attention,
Duchesse, you're getting mushy. Stop it this instant!

She looks at her bottle.

Ouais ben, the "siesta's" not over, but my bottle is empty . . . so that means that la Duchesse is going to find another one . . . And while she's at it, she'll also go and powder her nose . . . In other words, she's gonna go take a piss, like the most common of mortals . . .

She goes out "with dignity," albeit tipsy, the empty bottle under her arm. We hear a strong bass voice singing, "Take Me Out to the Ball Game."

Act Two

LA DUCHESSE makes her way back on stage, a bottle under one arm, a glass in one hand and an ice bucket in the other.

She is all dressed in white.

Dear Lord, make my heart as pure as thine! Ouf! Pissing only gets me more plastered . . . I can never understand it . . . I think I'm twice as bad as I was before . . .

She sets the bottle on the table.

Well, mon amour, if you get to the bottom of that one, it's not dead-drunk they're gonna find you, but drunk, dead! . . . I'm pooped just trying to open it.

She opens the bottle, pours herself a glass and starts in on the same routine as as the beginning.

Oh, shut up, everybody knows!

She drinks.

Mmmm! It's divine on the rocks! Can't stand it straight . . .

She looks into her glass and plays with the ice cubes.

Clink, clink, clink . . . That is the most charactis . . . characteristic sound of a woman of the world! The tinkle of ice cubes against the rim of a glass . . . When I hear that, I get the most wicked thoughts . . . You know something, my lambie pies, I have drunk whiskey in every conceivable, possible position.

Very woman of the world.

Mine is a life of ice cubes tinkling in whiskey glasses. Whiskey and men, they'll be my perdition!

She gives a big perverse smile à la Marilyn Monroe, a little cry and a toss of the hip.

At one time I used to drink whiskey with a straw 'cause it looked chic . . . But boy, does it get you plastered! And it tastes like shit! . . . Yes, for forty-odd years now, la Duchesse has been ingurgitating this miraculous liquid, which, as you have no doubt noticed, makes her so voluble and interesting . . . I say forty *odd* years because the first time I ever drank whiskey was when I was ten. It was my First Communion, and my big sister Laurette was trying to be funny . . . Me, I was sick as a dog . . .

Laughing.

For a little girl making her First Communion, I was horrible! What a pain! I was ugly as a monkey's ass scratched with two hands, my dress all crooked, and my eyes in cousin Léopold's pants. That's right. Already! People are always surprised when I tell them that, but what can I do, it's the God's truth. Cousin Léopold started on me when I was barely six years old. It's true! He didn't just go for the young ones, he went for the babies! What a crazy! He died in the nuthouse, you know . . . Really, and to the great shame of the whole family . . . Me, I've buried them all!

She drinks.

He sucked me so hard I'd have spasms and I'd scream 'cause it hurt so much. Of course I couldn't ejaculate, I was too young . . . I didn't even know what was happening to me . . . All I knew was not to say anything to anybody . . . But pretty soon I started getting a kick out of it anyway. I must admit, I was always a bit of a masochist . . . I love it when males hurt me! Sometimes I'd even tease cousin Léopold to make him crazy so he'd hurt me more . . . His eyes woud get all red and he'd come charging at me . . . Six years old! And already I was depraved!

She stares at the audience for sometime, then she goes to sit down.

I know, you're right. It's disgusting.

She pauses.

Yeah, well, la Duchesse would rather not think about that now because la Duchesse too has started running after the kids!

She pounds her fist down on the table.

Oh! Oh! Temper, temper! Don't break anything, dear, especially your pretty little hand. You're still going to need that . . . Here, have another drink and you'll forget all about it.

She drinks.

After all, you're still a woman of the world! So pull yourself together. If you can't make it anymore, you can go back for your fourth face lift and die on the operating table.

She drinks again.

Later on, after cousin Léopold, when I started to enjoy it, I'd let people feel me up at the show . . . Boy, did I love that! I'd sit near some guy who looked like he'd go and I'd stare at him . . . When he'd get the picture, he'd come and sit next to me . . . I was so excited, I'd shake like a leaf . . . He'd rub his knee against mine . . .

She wipes her hand across her brow.

How old was I then? . . . Maybe twelve . . . We'd usually go finish up in the toilets . . . Sometimes we'd go to his place, but not very often. Men were always scared 'cause I was so young. I was dangerous!

Suddenly changing her tone.

But, darling, you have always been dangerous. And you still are!

She pours herself a drink.

So that means that I've done without men for five years of my life . . . the first five.

She makes a face and drinks. She looks worn-out and crushed, like a drunken old whore. Suddenly, she reacts.

I want a Peruvian sailor in my bed tonight! I've just decided and I won't go to bed until I've got a Peruvian sailor by the tail . . . That will get all these nasty things off my mind.

Very woman of the world.

I've always adored sailors. They're my weak point, vous savez?

Speaking naturally.

For a while I kept a record of my sailors . . . I stopped at two hundred and thirty-eight . . . I lost my notebook . . . It's unbelievable, the money I made with sailors. They must pay more than anyone else . . . It's no wonder, hein, they go for months without seeing a woman. I remember in New York, the whores hated me . . . Of course, I can't blame them, hein, I stole all their meat . . . Of course too, I was a lot more woman than they were!

She gets up with a stagger, her two arms in the air.

I've always been more woman than all the women!

She falls back into her chair.

I think you'd better stay seated, dear, the floor wants you.

She pours a drink.

A toast . . . Yes, yes, a toast, Duchesse. You do it so well . . . I drink to the health of . . . My God, everything's all red. I am plastered . . . I drink to the health of . . . Once at a party at the end of the war, I came in nude, my body all covered with Heinz ketchup. I was the widow of the Unknown Soldier . . . What a success! I made quite a mess of Monsieur's maison,

but that didn't matter . . . It seems they even found
ketchup on the handle of a vacuum cleaner . . .

She breaks out laughing.

What was I saying? . . . Oh yes!

She gets up with difficulty.

I drink to the health of l'amour with a capital "A."

She drinks and sits down again.

Peter! Peter! I don't believe it.

> *She tries to get up. Unable to make it, she puts
> her forehead on the table. She tries to speak
> rapidly, but the words get all mixed up and she
> stutters.*

A Peruvian sailor! I need a Peruvian sailor with his
pants full of goods, a big bundle of goods that I can
grab with both hands!

She lifts her head but keeps her eyes shut.

Yes, with both hands! Then ally-up, into the sack.

She opens her eyes.

Let me tell you something . . . Even if I've started to
look like an old bag, a man doesn't get bored with me
in bed. Far from it! Oh no! La Duchesse is still more
than capable of out-performing the children of today.
La technique is still there, my darlings, it's all in la
technique. Just tell your aunt what you'd like and
she'll take care of the rest. She'll even give you a
little extra, free of charge! Private little tricks that
nobody knows. That is, nobody but la Duchesse!

She closes her eyes.

Come with me, lover boy, come with me for the time
of your life. Show me your pecker so your aunt can
gobble it up.

She opens her eyes.

I've got such control. I can pucker it up for a kiss.
Yes, I've taken lots of shit. But only because I wanted
to! Because I like it! Because I like to please whoever
I make love to.

She jumps up.

Never say that word again, Duchesse. Never again.

She sits down.

Say "fuck" all you want, but never that word. From
now on, my darlings, your woman of the world is
going to fuck and that's all.

She leans her head on the table and murmurs.

La Duchesse de Langeais has a broken . . .

She raises her head.

Cunt! That's right, and you'll just have to get used
to it. To think that at sixty years of age you have to
change your vocabulaire because of some shitty little
worm! I met him right around here, in one of the
cafés. I asked him, with a little pout, naturellement,
what he liked to do in bed? I mean, a woman of the
world is a woman of the world. He looked me straight
in the eye and said, "I'm a fucking buck-driver-
buffalo!" I almost had a haemorrhage! I was frothing
at the ass! In the wink of an eye, we threw ourselves
into each other's arms . . . I wasn't at all prepared for
what happened to me. I thought I'd been immune to

27

that bug for ages! You can sure fool yourself, hein?
You go along thinking you have no heart left, and
then, pow, you wake up to discover that that's all
there is. Within three days I was madly in love. I'd
have done anything for him . . . And he'll be twenty
years old next month.

A long silence.

Ever since then, I've been taking care of him. I feed
him, I wash him . . . Oh, he loves it when I wash
him . . . I take him out, I wipe his nose, I run along
before him . . . Yeah, I run in front of him because I
love him! I love the little bastard. Why shouldn't I
say it? That hasn't happened to me for forty years!

Very woman of the world.

I guess that's what they call "décadence!" Love with
a capital "L." I have reigned for too long a time
not to know how revolting it is to stoop before
someone . . . and to serve . . . But I can't help it.
I'm in love like an eighteen year old girl who's still
got her cherry. And it's not even 'cause he's good
in bed! 'Cause he isn't! I don't know what it is, I
don't know! But I can't stand being without him.
It's . . . It's as if he were my child . . . What I feel
for him is almost pure!

A long silence.

He's been gone since yesterday. He left me a goodbye
note! A polite little "mot d'adieu!" To me, la Duchesse!
No man has ever run out on me. Never! Oh, I've made
lots of them suffer, but nobody could ever brag about
having made me cry. Well, I bawled like a teeny-
bopper all night long! Can you believe it? And if
he doesn't come back, I know I'm gonna die like an
old bitch.

Silence.

I know he won't come back . . .

She pours herself a drink and drinks it.

If the vacationing CBC girls could see me now, they'd be happy as pigs in shit. I don't care. I'll never sober up!

Very woman of the world.

Let them say what they like.

Silence.

And what's more, he left me for some eighteen year old beauty. A "native" that he found along the beach! Duchesse, your pride should rise up in your throat and choke you to death! After two bottles of whiskey you haven't got much pride left, hein, ma chérie? Everything's flown the coop. Even your fake love for Peruvian sailors has taken off ass-end over tea cups. Now suffer, you bitch! It's your own fault. Paye, ma câlice, paye! You're always bragging about your forty years experience. So why didn't you do what experience taught you? So, die, goddamn it! Die! Don't try to fight it. It's no use.

Silence.

Very woman of the world.

Sure, I know, nobody dies for love nowadays . . . but when they find my body . . . That's a pile of shit, Duchesse, and you know it. You're not going to die and that's what's so horrible. Ben oui, it hurts, but it will pass. You've seen worse, you know. Fini, l'amour. It's all in the past. Have a good cry, roll around on the floor if you want, then . . . Then, do like you've always done . . . Tell yourself you're the most beautiful, the most élégant, and that the world is full of men waiting for you.

She struggles to her feet.

The men are at your feet, Duchesse!

She falls heavily onto the table.

Who gives a shit? I don't want them anymore.

The bottle gets knocked over, splashing LA DUCHESSE in the face. She doesn't move.

They call me "la Duchesse de Langeais" because I've always dreamed that I'd die a Carmelite nun . . . sipping tea!

Berthe

*BERTHE is enthroned in her glass ticket window
at the chic cabaret, "The Coconut Inn." She is
well over forty.*

*BERTHE is enthroned in her glass ticket window
at the chic cabaret, "The Coconut Inn." She is
well over forty. (One might also say there is still
a glimmer of what she was in the Forties.) She
wears very "stylish" glasses made of blue plastic
and shaped like cat's eyes, liberally sprinkled
with "diamond dust." She is reading a movie
magazine and drinking a cream soda with two
straws.*

*It is night, during the eleven o'clock show. The
doorman can be heard calling, "Showtime!
Showtime!" four or five times.*

BERTHE:
   Not many people tonight, eh? . . .

31

She drinks.

Of course, Wednesday night . . . Especially with the stars we've got this week! There's not even a hundred people . . .

She suddenly closes her magazine.

What a bore! What a bore! And there'll be no more customers now until the next show.

DOORMAN:
Showtime! Showtime!

BERTHE:
Will you shut up, the show's already started! God, what a pain! Day in, day out, "Showtime! Showtime!" That's all he ever does, is stand there and yell "Showtime! Showtime!"

Speaking louder so the DOORMAN will hear her.

You know, you really gotta be stupid, eh, to . . .

She suddenly stops and returns angrily to her cream soda.

Bloody moron, he can't even put two words together! At least the other one used to come shoot the breeze once in a while. But him, what a dope! . . . "Showtime! Showtime!" He's gonna drive me nuts! It's bad enough being locked up in here . . .

She leafs through her magazine.

You're not locked up, Berthe. You're not locked up. You're just waiting . . . Of course, meanwhile in Hollywood, they get married, they get divorced, they're in the big time . . . They get paid a million bucks a movie! Can you believe it? A million bucks for one movie! And they squawk 'cause there's only a few hundred thousand left after the taxes.

She stops at one page.

The big time . . . Boy, are they lucky, those movie stars. And I bet you they don't even know it! Wow! Will you look at the fancy get up! What a life! . . . And me . . .

DOORMAN:
Showtime! Showtime!

BERTHE:
How long, dear God, how long?

She pauses.

If I could at least go in and watch the shows!

She goes back to her magazine.

Sometimes I wonder . . . I look at them there and I ask myself, "What do they have that I haven't got?"

She closes her eyes.

"Oh, Sister, you ought to take Berthe. She's a very good actress."

DOORMAN:
Showtime! Showtime!

BERTHE:
Today it's selling tickets. Yesterday . . . Tomorrow . . . How long, dear God, how long?

She drinks.

You've no right to complain, Berthe! There are lots of people who work harder than you and for less money! You're lucky! It's a privilege! All you have to do is sit in the window and sell tickets. That's easy enough! There's nothing to it . . . You can read . . .

She looks at her magazine, disgusted.

Oh God, I'm so bored!

DOORMAN:
Showtime! Showtime!

BERTHE:
If you've got a doorman who'll come and talk to you . . . that helps pass the time . . .

She smiles bitterly.

"Showtime! Showtime!" . . . And you just sit here . . .

She closes her eyes.

Get up, Berthe! Come on, get up. Do something!

She opens her eyes again.

Why do I stay here, it's so boring?

DOORMAN:
Showtime! Showtime!

BERTHE:
What am I doing with my life? I could . . .

She pauses.

I've been to school . . . ninth grade . . . I'm no worse than the next guy . . . I could . . . I could . . .

She drinks.

Didn't I tell you, Sister, Berthe is a very good actress! A very good actress, a very good actress . . . A good actress . . ." "Yes, and I'm so glad I chose her for this scene . . . She's by far the best and most beautiful Thérèse de l'Enfant Jésus that we've ever had . . . The best and the most beautiful . . . That child will go far if she wants to!" Those actors, it's only 'cause they're lucky! All you need is one stroke of luck and you've made it . . . A star! And all the rest of it! And you make millions while some people . . .

She looks around her.

Not all actors are so beautiful. Me too, with a ton of make-up on my face . . .

Defeated, she goes back to her cream soda.

"That child will go far if she wants to . . ." "Of course he's a nice boy, Berthe, of course . . . A very nice boy . . . But why don't you wait a while . . . You deserve better than that . . . Wait a few years before you decide. You're too young! You've gotta think before you settle down for good . . ." No, that's not how it happened! That can't be how it happened! When I finished school . . .

With affectation.

When I finished school, I met a young man who was going to . . . to the Conservatory! Yes, yes, that's it, to the Conservatory of Theatre! An excellent actor! He introduced me to his friends . . . A wonderful group . . . All of them excellent actors . . . Right away, I became . . . Oh, how do you say it? . . . Oh yes! Right away, I became the darling of the group. All the men were running after me. I had countless affairs! Countless, countless affairs . . . And one day, a director noticed me . . . I was . . . Yes, yes, that's it . . . It was at a big party at some well known actress' place . . . Oh, what was her name? . . . Who do I usually think of now when I get to this part . . . She's so well known . . . Anyway . . . I was . . . standing in front of a window . . . Oh yes, it's so much nicer that way! I was standing in front of a window . . . I had on a green dress . . . Long? Oh yes, long! A long green dress! I was . . . drinking champagne! The minute he saw me, he came running over and asked me to take the leading role in his new play . . . Of course I said yes . . . What a success! . . . How do they say that? . . . Ah, yes, a phenomenal success! "You're too beautiful, Berthe. You're too beautiful to shut yourself up in a house and start raising kids right away. You deserve better than that. Wait little longer . . . Stop and think about it before you decide for life." I was beautiful! I was chosen Miss Radio right away, the first year! And ever since then . . . ever since then there isn't a role that I haven't played . . . "Madame Bovary" . . . "La Duchesse de Langeais" . . . That's Balzac. "La Dame aux Camélias!" I've played "La Dame aux Camélias" all over the world! That's what made me famous!

She pauses.

I'm famous the world over . . . I'm famous . . . I am . . .

Very softly.

. . . the most famous actress in the world!

Loudly.

It's true!

Silence. She looks slowly around her.

"Someday you're going to thank me, Berthe! When you're surrounded with thousands of fans . . . When you'll be famous . . . Yes, yes, yes, you can become a great and famous actress if you work. You're beautiful enough, and good enough . . . All you have to do is take some courses . . . And with a little bit of luck . . . You remember, at school, the Sisters always said so! They always chose you to play in the skits." "What a life I've led! But if I'm where I am today, it's because I've worked. I've worked hard! You have to work to become a great actress! Come on, Berthe. Get up! Get up, Berthe. Get going. Get a move on! Do something! It's now or never! Time is flying, Berthe. You've got to make up your mind . . ."

DOORMAN:
Showtime! Showtime!

In a fit of panic, BERTHE suddenly turns around to look behind her toward the door of her ticket booth.

BERTHE:
Is the door there?

She slowly returns to her initial position.

That's silly to get scared like that . . .

She drinks.

"Look, it's high time you decide to do something, eh, Berthe? 'Cause time's flying! You're making good money with the job you've got, but you're worth more than that. When you get to be your age there's only one way out . . ." No, no, that's not how it happened! I'm the greatest actress in the world and I get a million bucks per movie! I'm not locked up in this box!

DOORMAN:
Showtime! Showtime!

BERTHE:
I'm not locked up in this box!

She looks around her.

How long, dear God, how long? If I can't dream, I'm gonna suffocate.

A long silence, then coldly.

The other cashier got sick and there was nobody else to replace her, so I started right away the next morning . . . And that was . . . how many years ago? No, I'd rather not think about it! "You're lucky, a nice easy job!"

She pauses.

A whole life spent selling tickets in a glass box!

Very loudly.

My God!

She pauses.

I know it's too late. I know there's nothing I can do. Everyone's been telling me for years. But let them say what they want. I'm not that crazy! "You're nothing but a bloody dreamer," they tell me. "All you're good for is making up crazy stories that don't make any sense! We never know if you're telling the truth or if you're dreaming outloud. If you keep going like that, you're going to find yourself without any friends, Berthe. One of these days you're going to wind up alone! All by yourself!" Do something, Berthe. Do something!

A long silence.

But I never did anything.

A long silence.

I don't ask for much now . . . Just let me have my dreams. Leave me in peace and let me dream! That's all I've got left. 'Cause I do know how to dream. Ha! Do I ever! Maybe I'm dumb, but that doesn't keep me from making up stories. I know I don't look it, but I can make up, all for myself, the real life of a real Hollywood star. I'm not too smart, but I know how to make myself think I am. So what if I look stupid sittting here, I could have done something with my life if I'd wanted to.

She pauses.

But I never did anything. I just sat here in my box.

She pauses.

And if I dream that someday I'll get out of my box, or that I never even got in it, so what? I don't bother anyone. I still do my job. And if I don't dream, I'm gonna suffocate! It's all I've got left!

A long silence.

Sure, I know I'll never get out of here . . . I know it . . . They'll have to carry me out. I'm too old. My life is over. Berthe, your life is over! You spent your whole life waiting, but nothing ever came! It's winter, Berthe! "Oh, Sister, you should take Berthe. She's a very good actress! Besides, she doesn't mind rehearsing with you while the rest of us go skating . . . She's a real artist." It's winter now . . . No, I mustn't think about that. If I do, I'll go crazy.

She pauses.

It's so long! It's so long! And so boring.

Johnny Mangano
& His Astonishing Dogs

A fairly roomy, but very dirty dressing room at the "Coconut Inn." To the right, the door. It opens to the inside and whenever anyone comes in or out, a gold star can be seen hanging on the door. Written in sequins across it is the word "STAR". Beneath it, there is a little sign which says "JOHNNY MANGANO."

To the left, there is a make-up table with the usual light bulbs, lipsticks, photos of the "stars," kleenex boxes, and assorted bric-a-brac for make-up. There is an old, torn folding screen masking one corner of the dressing room.

In the centre, there is a huge poster upon which we see JOHNNY MANGANO in person, accompanied by his seven or eight dogs of various breeds and one monkey. They are all smiling. The inscription, "Johnny Mangano and His Astonishing Dogs," is seen in big red letters.

Loud laughter and guffaws can be heard coming from the audience, then applause and whistling.

41

All this is backed up by the final measures of some South American tune.

M.C.:

There they are, ladies and gentlemen! Aren't they gorgeous? Et voilà, mesdames et messieurs, ne sont-ils pas gorgeux? Come on, folks. Let's hear it, une bonne main d'applaudissements! A good hand for our stars! Johnny Mangano and His Astonishing Dogs! Johnny Mangano et ses Etonnants Chiens! Thank you, Johnny, you are the most! Vous l'avez, l'affaire, continuez! Isn't that so, ladies and gentlemen, aren't they the greatest?

Applause.

Right . . . C'est ça . . .

CARLOTTA bursts into the dressing room and slams the door behind her. She goes straight to the make-up table, takes a cigarette from a soft pack and nervously lights it. The applause has stopped.

CARLOTTA is dressed like all girls who appear in "performing dog numbers." She is wearing the usual sequined costume with feathers on the seat — a beautiful outfit of shiny cloth and ostrich feathers — and a rhinestone diamond. She is between two ages (which is to say she is precisely forty years old), a strawberry blond and is ultra made-up in the worst showbiz sense of the word. She leans against the make-up table and wipes a hand across her forehead.

CARLOTTA:

I'm gonna kill him! So help me, God, I'm gonna find a knife and kill him!

A dog barks outside the dressing room.

JOHNNY: *offstage*
> No, Kiki, you're not coming in tonight . . . Be a
> good girl and go back in your cage . . . Carlotta's
> too tired . . .

> *KIKI barks.*

> I said no, Kiki! Now, lie down! Lie down, Sugar, or
> I'll give you a spanking.

CARLOTTA: *shrugging her shoulders*
> "I'll give you a spanking!" To a dog!

> *JOHNNY enters. He is the same age as
> CARLOTTA. He looks pleased and is in good
> form. He also wears the traditional dog trainer
> costume — the tuxedo. He leaves the door
> open behind him.*

JOHNNY.
> I'm gonna leave the door open so Kiki won't bark . . .

CARLOTTA:
> Yes, the poor thing. Her lungs are so weak. If she
> barks, she might get sick!

> *JOHNNY approaches CARLOTTA and kisses
> her back.*

JOHNNY:
> How're you doing, Sugar? You seemed a bit nervous
> tonight . . .

CARLOTTA:
> Keep your "Sugars" for Kiki and don't touch me!

JOHNNY:
> Well, pardon me! I won't come closer than three feet
> until you give me the word. Madame is somewhat
> aloof tonight?

CARLOTTA:

No, Madame is not aloof! Madame is fed up! She's
fed up to here! You expect me to be calm with
lighting like that? It's a regular fireworks display.
We never know what's coming next.

JOHNNY:

Ah, you'll get used to it . . . Anyway, you know it by
now, we've done it three times . . .

CARLOTTA:

Yeah, but the dogs need more time. You're gonna
drive them batty. Didn't you see how hard it was for
me to control them tonight? They're not used to
lights flashing in their faces all through the show.
Red, then blue, then yellow, pink, you name it,
all over the place. You can't even see where you're
going!

JOHNNY:

Oh, come on . . .

CARLOTTA:

We were a lot better off with plain lights, Johnny!
It's not a striptease we're doing, we're dog trainers.
And what's more, I got all the green spots! I can just
imagine how I look in green.

JOHNNY:

You're blowing things up again. It's fabulous from
the house. The waiters told me. And you heard the
applause we got.

CARLOTTA:

Yeah, well maybe it was for the lights and not us.
Look, those guys missed my exit again, it's the
third time. It's obvious even they get lost in you're
goddamned colours. My exit was pitch black. After
all kinds of colours for the dogs, your Carlotta goes

off in complete darkness and almost knocks her brains out on that big steel door in the wings. It's crazy!

JOHNNY: *laughing*
> So that's why you didn't take your curtain call. You're jealous. If you were a dancer and the main act, you wouldn't mind the lights. You'd want them all for yourself, then!

CARLOTTA:
> If I was a dancer and the main act, things would be a lot different. I'd choose my own lights. And there wouldn't be any of that sick green!

> *CARLOTTA absentmindedly starts chewing her nails.*

JOHNNY:
> Don't chew your nails, you know I hate that. How many times do I have to tell you? It can show up from the house. A woman with chewed nails looks ugly on stage . . . Besides, it's bad manners.

CARLOTTA:
> Will you listen to that. Mind your own business. When I don't have any nails left, I'll buy some new ones, okay? Besides, it's not my nails people look at.

JOHNNY:
> That's for sure! Did you see the second table on the left tonight? The guy's eyes were popping out of his head.

CARLOTTA:
> And I'm hardly the star of the show. Far from it.

JOHNNY:
> So what, a good looking girl always helps. I've always said it, "With a good looking chic on your arm, you

can walk through any door." I think I read that someplace . . .

CARLOTTA:
> I bet they never even saw me in my real colours. Oh, maybe once when I walked into Kiki's spot by mistake.

JOHNNY:
> A nightclub act without nice broads is like *Playboy* with no pictures. It's incomplete. If people don't like the act, at least the broad can hold their attention . . .

CARLOTTA:
> Come right out and say it, I'm just a prop!

JOHNNY:
> I see everything, you know. When I walked out there with Shirley, one look at the audience and I got 'em all sized up.

CARLOTTA:
> You don't say . . .

JOHNNY:
> And when Kiki makes her big entrance with you, their eyes are like saucers! Not always because of Kiki either!

CARLOTTA:
> Thanks a lot . . .

JOHNNY:
> Well, with legs like yours . . .

CARLOTTA:
> With legs like mine, if I hadn't followed you around all my life, I'd be a lot further than this, okay? It's me who'd be the star tonight!

JOHNNY:

> Of course, once they start looking at the rest, their
> faces drop fast, eh?

CARLOTTA:

> That's right, laugh at me! Keep right on laughing at
> me! That's all you ever do, isn't it? I suppose you're
> gonna tell me those lights tonight were so people
> could see me less!

JOHNNY:

> Come on, I'm only teasing. Don't get all in a flap.
> If you hate the green spot so much, I'll change it . . .
> I'll give you a nice blue one!

CARLOTTA:

> You think you're smart, eh? I was just telling myself
> I'd find me a knife and kill you . . . I still might do
> it . . .

JOHNNY:

> Hey, what is this? What's the matter with you?
> You're in a shitty mood tonight. Is it a bad time of
> the month or something?

CARLOTTA:

> You've pretty well lost track of my times of the
> month, eh?

JOHNNY:

> Now wait a minute! You're not gonna tell me I've
> been ignoring you lately? I'm faithful as a dog.

CARLOTTA:

> Dogs again! There's no end to it! Maybe you're
> faithful as a dog, Johnny, but there are times when
> you leave me alone for days on end and you go blow
> what little money we have left.

JOHNNY:

> What's that supposed to mean?

CARLOTTA:
Come on, Johnny, I'm not stupid. When you
disappear for the whole day, like you did today,
you don't think I know where you're going? I wasn't
born yesterday. Maybe I'm just a prop in the act,
but I'm a little smarter than the dogs. I haven't
mentioned it for a long time, I haven't made any
scenes, but don't think for a minute I don't know
what's going on.

JOHNNY:
So what if I go out for the afternoon, every once in
a while? I've always done that . . . Look, as long as
I come back at night . . .

CARLOTTA:
Yeah, just in time for the show . . . Listen, Johnny,
the money's disappearing and it's not coming back.
And it's getting serious. You're still losing at cards,
aren't you? Well, it's about time you learned how to
win! It's been long enough! And what's more, I'm
sick of spending my days with the dogs. I'd like to
see people too, you know. We've been back in
Montréal for two days, and you've already seen all
your friends and you've even lost at cards, just like
the good old days . . . But what about me, eh? Who
have I seen since we got back? The old bag in the
ticket booth who was there when we left twelve
years ago! I haven't even called my mother 'cause
I know she'll ask me to go and see her, but I'd have
to say no 'cause I couldn't leave the dogs alone!

JOHNNY:
Come on, Carlotta, you're making a fuss over
nothing . . .

CARLOTTA:
Don't call me Carlotta! I've asked you a thousand
times not to call me Carlotta when we're alone!
My name is Charlotte, Johnny! Charlotte Toupin!

48

I know it's ugly, but too bad! It's my name and
that's what I want to be called. It's not my fault
I was born with it!

JOHNNY:

That's the whole point. There's no reason you should
die with it. Especially in showbiz. I think "Carlotta"
is nice . . .

CARLOTTA:

Well, I think Carlotta sounds cheap! I'm not an
Italian! I was born in Montréal. My father's name was
Octave Toupin and he was a plumber!

JOHNNY:

Yeah, yeah, I know, but can't you understand . . .
When you became an artist . . .

CARLOTTA:

Artists? Us? My father the plumber was more of
an artist than we are. Don't be ridiculous. Listen,
Johnny Mangano, the great dog trainer, I've got
showbiz in my blood, in my legs, and I knew it the
first minute I ever got on a stage . . . If it hadn't
been for you, I could have become a real star. With
a little work, I could have been a great dancer!

JOHNNY:

You don't know the first thing about dancing.

CARLOTTA:

Go on, laugh. I don't care . . . I've been telling you
for years that I want to take dance lessons . . . But
no . . . The dogs, nothing but the dogs . . . Who needs
dancing? . . . Well, as for your "showbiz," in the
twelve years that we've been away, we've seen plenty
of it and we've had lots of time to see that the big
music hall stars are artists, real ones! And there're
lots of good dog numbers, too. Christ, there're
thousands of them! But let me tell you, the stuff
that we're doing . . .

JOHNNY:

> Look, Charlotte, we're billed as American stars in one of the biggest clubs in Montréal! We're just as good as any other artists! What more do you want?

CARLOTTA:

> I don't believe it! "What more do I want?" I want less, Johnny.

> *Suddenly she goes to the door and closes it.*

> Have you forgotten what I told you yesterday? You want me to make a scene? Well, that's what I'm gonna do!

JOHNNY:

> Oh no! You're not gonna start that again? Look, Carlotta, it's time you got something straight . . .

CARLOTTA:

> Speak French when you talk to me! You know I don't understand English and I don't want to understand it!

JOHNNY: *grabbing her wrist*

> Hey! I'll talk to you in whatever language I like, and you're gonna understand, okay? You're starting to get on my nerves! Now you'll get this through your head, even if I say it in Chinese! Who's boss around here?

CARLOTTA: *pulling away*

> The dogs!

JOHNNY:

> What? What's that supposed to mean?

CARLOTTA:

> Nothing, I was talking to myself . . .

> *KIKI barks.*

JOHNNY:
>I told you, the door's gotta stay open! Now Kiki's barking again.

>*CARLOTTA smiles.*

>If only you'd let her in the dressing room like before. That dog is unhappy and it's your fault. She doesn't bother anything in here . . .

CARLOTTA:
>She's a bloody pain!

JOHNNY:
>Why, all she does is walk around . . .

CARLOTTA:
>Johnny, shut your yap!

>*JOHNNY looks at her, surprised.*

>Oh, it works with you, too? I'll have to try that more often. Listen to me, Johnny, and listen good. I'm gonna talk to you very calmly . . . For the hundredth time I'm going to tell you what I've been telling you every night for the last three months . . . I don't want Kiki in the dressing room anymore. I can't stand her anymore. Now can you get that through your head once and for all? I can't stand looking at her.

JOHNNY:
>But why?

CARLOTTA:
>I've know the bitch for twelve years, Johnny! For twelve years, I've been tripping over her!

JOHNNY:
>What are you talking about, tripping over her for twelve years?

CARLOTTA:

> Johnny, we've known one another for twelve years.

JOHNNY:

> So what's that supposed to mean? Hey, you're not gonna compare me to Kiki, are you?

CARLOTTA:

> Johnny, for twelve years you haven't compared me, even to that bitch! Never mind, don't bother, I know you don't understand . . . You'll never understand . . . I didn't mean to compare you to Kiki, Johnny. I was just hoping to show you something as plain as the nose on your face . . . But it's not worth the trouble . . .

JOHNNY:

> Sure, come right out and say it. I'm retarded!

CARLOTTA: *very softly*

> No, you're not retarded. You're just slow to catch on . . . You're just a little bit thick . . .

JOHNNY:

> What? I didn't hear you . . .

CARLOTTA:

> Nothing, nothing . . . I'm talking to myself . . .

JOHNNY: *openly changing the subject*

> Well, we made quite a hit tonight, eh? Did you hear that applause, that whistling? Hey, we've got star billing, Charlotte. That's nothing to laugh at!

CARLOTTA:

> Dear God, he's gonna drive me nuts! If we've got star billing, Johnny, it's because the real star had an accident!

JOHNNY:

> You always look at the bad side of things.

CARLOTTA:

I'm just being realistic, Johnny. It's not me who's floating around in pink and yellow lights! I'm in the green! If we're the second act tonight, it's only because the real second act sprained her ankle. An acrobat without an ankle isn't worth much so you replace it with a performing dog routine that should be on third.

JOHNNY:

But this could be our big break! Especially since people seemed to like it. I'm telling you, there aren't many dogs like Kiki around. The little bugger . . . There's no stopping her . . . She understands everything . . . Just like that . . . You know, she might be the oldest dog in showbiz . . . And the smartest!

CARLOTTA:

Do you ever listen to yourself when you talk about that mutt? You sound like a newlywed.

JOHNNY:

Oh! That reminds me.

He runs out of the room. CARLOTTA sits down at the make-up table. She puts her forehead down on the table.

CARLOTTA:

He's gonna bring me Kiki's wedding dress that she tore during the show.

JOHNNY returns holding the dog's costume.

JOHNNY:

I don't know if you noticed, but Kiki tore her dress during the show . . . You'll have to sew it up, Charlotte . . . And the second show's gonna start pretty soon . . . I've been thinking, maybe we ought to buy her a new one, eh? This one's getting kind of shabby . . .

CARLOTTA:

> And me, when do I get my new costume? This thing
> is in rags!

JOHNNY:

> Charlotte! You're costumes cost a fortune!

CARLOTTA:

> Just let me remind you that Kiki's dress is real lace,
> while mine is cheap satin!

>> *JOHNNY doesn't answer. He puts the dress
>> down on the make-up table and goes towards
>> the arm chair in the centre of the room. He
>> starts reading the newspaper.*

JOHNNY:

> I'm gonna see if we got a review . . . We only started
> yesterday, but you never know . . .

CARLOTTA:

> Johnny, they have never talked about us in the
> papers!

JOHNNY:

> We haven't been in Montréal for a long time, Charlotte,
> maybe they cover the clubs here . . .

> *Leafing through the paper.*

> Hey, Charlotte, there's no entertainment section . . .

CARLOTTA:

> Look under "Arts et Lettres," Johnny. If they talk
> about us, it'll be under "Arts et Lettres."

>> *She takes KIKI's dress and looks at it for a long
>> time.*

Jesus Bloody Christ! To think that I spent twelve years in exile to wind up right back here! What a joke! I'm telling you, Johnny, it's a real joke.

JOHNNY doesn't answer.

Hey, goddamn it, I'm telling you how I've wasted my life sewing up wedding dresses for dogs! Now come on, Johnny, I want you to force yourself to try and understand. Don't you see how hilarious it is? Come on, laugh! Double up, roll on the floor! For twelve years I've followed you like a dog, Johnny. For twelve years I've been going on stage to play the girlie behind your other dogs and I've been showing off my legs to make people clap harder, now don't you think that's a riot? And everytime one of your stupid dogs does one of its stupid somersaults, I take a bow for it and I throw kisses! Now honestly, doesn't that make you piss your pants? And when the dogs go parading around as bride and groom and mom and dad and the monkey jumps out dressed like Uncle Sam waving the American flag, us, the human beings, we get behind them and we take the bows. Me in my cheap satin costume that I've been wearing for four years, and you in your fancy tails. You're dressed like the monkey, Johnny, did you ever notice that? We've been in this business for twelve years and in twelve years we've been through I don't know how many dogs. Dogs are our whole life, doesn't that make you die laughing? We don't buy new clothes 'cause the dogs need beautiful costumes. We don't go out 'cause we can't leave the dogs alone. We can't be alone together for ten minutes 'cause Kiki will bark! Our life is full of Kiki, Johnny, there's nothing else, there's nothing but Kiki in our life! That's all I've ever known for twelve years is dogs!

JOHNNY: *shouting*
Then why the hell did you follow me twelve years ago? Why didn't you stay home?

A long silence. CARLOTTA looks at JOHNNY in amazement. For a long time she looks him right in the eyes. Then she comes back and sits down at the make-up table.

Well, why didn't you? I didn't force you to come with me, Charlotte. When I wanted to start training dogs, I knew there was no future in Canada, so I decided to go to the States . . .

CARLOTTA:
Oh, you've got a funny memory.

JOHNNY:
You didn't have to come with me. Did I ask you to come? I sure as hell didn't! I wanted to go alone! You tied yourself to me, bawling your eyes out for days on end. I could have found broads like you by the hundreds in the States, and a lot better looking, too! If you came with me, it's because you wanted to come. So stop your bloody complaints. Without me and Kiki, you're nothing, Charlotte.

CARLOTTA:
I beg your pardon . . .

JOHNNY:
What would you do if I let you go, eh? What would you do? You couldn't even be a hooker, you're too old! Sure, you've still got nice legs, but you could never work up your own number, you'd be all out of breath. You'd probably wind up in a pet shop, 'cause all you know is animals. Is that what you want to do, live out your days selling dogs, cats and little birdies? Eh? Is that it? Well, go ahead. And just try going home to your place. Your old lady would have a field day. You'd be crawling back here in no time. All you know how to do, Charlotte, is to raise dogs and play the "girlie" on stage, so just do it and shut up!

CARLOTTA: *very lowly*
> To think I married that because I loved him . . . That
> I sacrificed everything because I loved him . . .

JOHNNY:
> What?

CARLOTTA:
> And to think I still love him . . .

JOHNNY:
> Speak up, for Chrissake, I can't hear you!

CARLOTTA:
> I'm talking to myself, Johnny, I'm talking to myself
> . . . And what I've got to say is not very interesting . . .

JOHNNY:
> You've been talking to yourself a little too often,
> lately. If you're gonna crack up, go see a doctor! And
> hurry up with Kiki's dress, the show starts in half an
> hour . . . There's nothing in the paper, but there
> might be reporters in the house! We've gotta be
> careful. We've got star billing, so the show's gotta
> be good! And I invited my buddies to the second
> show . . . I told 'em it was the best one . . . We'll
> spot 'em in the crowd . . . You'll see, Charlotte,
> you'll see.

> *CARLOTTA throws the dress on the table and*
> *gets up.*

CARLOTTA:
> Now, hold it right there! I want you to listen to me.
> I want you to listen for two minutes without butting
> in, okay? I've got something very important to tell
> you . . . That's right, of the most earth-shaking
> importance. You say you want me to shut up, eh?
> Well I want you to shut up and I want you to stop
> dreaming in technicolour, so I'm gonna get this off
> my chest once and for all!

She slams the door with all her might.

And let Kiki howl all she wants. It'll do her good!
Now, you want to know what our act is worth,
Johnny, eh, you want me to tell you what it's worth?
It's worth zero, a great big zero with a capital "Z!"
Our act is terrible, Johnny. It's ridiculous!

JOHNNY:

Hey, that's a bit much, isn't it?

CARLOTTA:

Shut up! Let me finish! Maybe our act used to be
good, but we've been doing it for twelve years. The
same act for twelve years! So it's starting to lose it's
shine, you know what I mean? Christ, we had to
come back to Montréal because they saw too much
of us in the States. But when we go back down there,
all we'll have to show them that's new is your Jell-O
bowl of lights! Look, I'll give you an example of
what I mean. Now you look at me, Johnny, look
me right in the eyes . . . Remember when you got it
into your head that we should go on television?
Eh? You remember that?

JOHNNY:

Yeah, and we got on television too.

CARLOTTA:

Oh, we got on television alright, did we ever! It
took us three years, but we got there. At least you
succeeded in doing that in your life. But you know,
I think you should have left well enough alone. We
got on once, but we've never been back. And that was
six years ago! And do you know why? It's because
we're no good! People who come to the clubs think
we're funny 'cause they're half-plastered and they get
a charge out of seeing a dog dressed up like a bride
and a monkey like Uncle Sam. But you can be
damned sure that the millions of people who saw
us on TV didn't find us so funny. Christ, you were

so nervous you hit one of the dogs with your whip
right on TV 'cause he wouldn't climb onto his stupid
balloon! You always spoil everything, Johnny. You're
just a dreamer and you'll always be a dreamer. When
you decided to become a dog trainer, it wasn't because
you didn't have a cent to your name. You were
twenty-eight years old and one of your buddies gave
you this bright idea. But you'd never accomplished
anything in your life. All you knew how to do was
to play pool and go to the races with other people's
money. And stupid me, I loved you. That's right,
I had the misfortune of meeting you in some pool
room door and falling in love with you even though
you were a bum who ran after every broad he ever
met. Remember that, Johnny Mangano, eh? Remember
when your name was still Jean Ladouceur and everybody'd laugh behind your back when you'd play the
tough guy? "Ladouceur, the big tough," they'd call
you. I haven't forgotten those days, Johnny, oh no,
I haven't forgotten them at all. You'd never made a
penny 'cause you were too much of a dreamer and
all you could think of was glory! Then one day, the
great inspiration, a regular fairy tale. One of your
buddies tells you he knows this dog trainer who's
got some dogs for sale, real cheap, and that's the
business you ought to be in. Three beers at the
tavern and you were already the biggest dog trainer
in America! Our whole life was decided in a tavern
around a table full of beers. Think about it, Johnny,
have you ever heard of anything so ridiculous? I
could write that to Ann Landers and she wouldn't
believe me! You knew nothing about dogs, Johnny.
And what's more, you went and bought the dumb
things on credit without even laying eyes on them.
You were already off in the clouds. You already saw
yourself a big star in the American clubs. But you
didn't know how many legs a dog has! That is why
I followed you when you decided to take off. I loved
you, Johnny, and I knew that if you left by yourself,
this time you'd break your neck but good. So just
dig around in your little head, sweetheart, and try

to remember what really happened. Stop telling yourself stories and get back down to earth, okay? Like, do you remember Providence, Rhode Island? Who was it that realized he didn't have the patience to put up with the mutts he'd bought? Who was it that said dogs made too much noise, that dogs got on his nerves?

JOHNNY:
Shut up, Carlotta!

CARLOTTA:
I'm not a dog, Johnny, you won't get me to shut up that easily.

JOHNNY lifts his arm to hit her.

And that won't shut me up either! Sit down and listen!

She shoves him back into his chair.

It had to happen, eh, the dogs you bought were all sick. Dead as doornails in two weeks. All but Kiki, Kiki the pisspot, the only one who didn't croak. My God, what a laugh! But who's the one who collapsed in the hotel room, bawling his eyes out because his life was a mess? Was it me or was it you? You couldn't stand dogs, you didn't have the patience, but you knew they'd make you a living because I'd take care of them, me, the idiot! Yeah, and who spent days trying to find a book on how to train dogs? Sure, you read it 'cause I didn't know English, but which one of us got it all together and taught Kiki her first tricks? Me, all by myself! Oh, she already knew a few little things, but she was nothing but a chorus girl with all those dead dogs. She'd never been a star! So it was me, Charlotte Toupin, daughter of a two-bit Montréal plumber, who taught her all she knows. That's right! It was me who made Kiki the chorus girl into Kiki the star! And it's me who taught you how to live with a ten month old dog, Johnny, and it's me who showed you how to train dogs. If I hadn't been there, you wouldn't have done a thing! And if I did all that, it's because I loved you and because we had too little money and too much pride to come back to Montréal right away. All I wanted was to do our little number for a while, just long enough to pay for our dead dogs, and then to come back to Montréal. But wouldn't you know it, it had to work. People had to go and like it! You remember the first time we got on stage? Between the two of us we had one dog to show off. Of course you already had your name on the posters, but I'm the only one Kiki would listen to. So I'm the one who, in addition to playing the girlie, had to make her do her stupid tricks. Boy, did you look dumb standing there with your whip. God knows why, but the crowd thought it was great. Maybe it was us and our pink poodle who were so funny and that's what made 'em laugh. Maybe they thought we were funnier than the dog . . . Anyway, we kept at it, and like it or not, I was stuck. Hell, it was the first time in your life you'd made any money. So we went and bought more dogs, ones that weren't sick, and a monkey. You even got so as you could put up with them, so as you could work with them. In fact, I'd go so far as to say that that's when you got your passion for animals. With you it's all or nothing, eh? One day you can't stand dogs and the next you're madly in love with them. And that, Johnny, is when you started taking better care of Kiki than you did me. We are far from being the best dog trainers in the States, as you say in our publicity. And maybe Kiki is the oldest dog in showbiz — as for being old, she's old — but she certainly isn't the smartest. She's probably the most ridiculous, but . . . Sometimes I look at her on stage and I see how ugly she is, I mean really ugly! I hate that dog, Johnny, I hate her. I can't even stand her on stage anymore. At times I want to trip her just so people will laugh at her. That

fat pink bitch dressed up like a young bride . . .
She makes me sick to my stomach. An old bitch,
dressed like a young bride, you know, Johnny, it
really is revolting. And to think you care more for
that than you do me.

> *JOHNNY gets up suddenly and slaps CARLOTTA.*
> *CARLOTTA doesn't move. She stares at him.*
> *JOHNNY makes a gesture of trying to take her*
> *in his arms, but she turns away from him and*
> *goes to sit down at the make-up table. The*
> *STAGE MANAGER sticks his head in the door.*

STAGE MANAGER:
Five minutes, Mister Mangano, five minutes.

JOHNNY:
Yeah, yeah, we'll be ready.

> *KIKI barks.*

Shut up, Kiki!

> *To the STAGE MANAGER.*

Goddamned dogs, they never stop yapping.

> *The STAGE MANAGER disappears. JOHNNY*
> *approaches CARLOTTA.*

Have you finished now?

CARLOTTA:
No, but I'm fed up. It's no good talking . . . What's
the use, we're stuck here, we'll stay here . . . Do you
see the end of the tunnel? I don't. Pitch black. Just
like my exits . . . We bash into the steel doors . . .

JOHNNY:
Look, Carlotta, that's all very nice, everything you
said. You've never said so much. And it's all very

clever 'cause this way you get to play the good part
. . . Oh, it may well be true, that whole bit about
how we got started, but there's something you left
out . . . You've only given one side of the story . . .

He leans over very closely to CARLOTTA's ear.

There's something you've forgotten, my lovely
Charlotte . . . If you followed me and never left me,
there must have been a reason . . . And couldn't it
be that you needed me as much as I needed you?

He caresses her.

Hmm? Couldn't it be that you never left me because
you didn't have the nerve? . . . You wanted me all to
yourself, Charlotte, and you did everything possible
to see that you got me! Everything! That's why you
started the act. So your cage, sweetie, you built it
yourself! And you're right, we're in it together and
we'll always be in it together. There's nothing that'll
get us out. Maybe you followed me around all your
life, but it was never for my sake, it was for yours.
And it's not my fault if you're not a dancer, Carlotta.
It's your fault, your own bloody fault. I know I'm
a bit of a sop sometimes, like now, when I let you
bawl me out, but I also know what I'm doing. Like,
I know your little fits always finish by running out
of steam . . . I'm not as stupid as I look, Charlotte.
It's you who needs me! And don't I know it!

He kisses her on the neck.

I'm gonna get the dogs ready. It's nice to fight once
in a while, but you've still gotta make a living, eh?
Gotta take care of our dogs and the monkey . . .

*He goes towards the door. Just before he goes
out, he turns to CARLOTTA.*

Kiki needs to be brushed before the show . . .

He goes out, KIKI barks.

Hello, my little cutie, how're you doing? . . . Yeah . . . We're gonna brush you now . . .

> *CARLOTTA picks up the bride's dress. She looks at herself in the mirror.*

CARLOTTA:
Yeah, yeah. Me too, I know all that . . . We're at the bottom of the barrel and we'll never get any higher. We'll go to the grave with our dogs and our monkey. They'll bring out the girlie in a wheelchair, but the dogs will still be doing their stuff. When Kiki dies, we'll make Shirley the bride and when Shirley dies, there'll be another one to take her place. And us, we'll be propped up there like a couple of old stiffs . . . We'll become old dog trainers. Hey, I'll have spent my whole life acting like an idiot on stage behind a dog that I'd like to strangle for the love of Jean Ladouceur, alias Johnny Mangano, who will have treated me like just another one of his dogs. I'll have spent my life training dogs that my husband likes more than he does me. And on top of that, it's my own fault. It's me who taught him to love dogs.

> *She gets up and goes to stand in front of the big poster.*

You fool! You stupid fool! "And His Astonishing Dogs." Me, I'm one of the "Astonishing Dogs!" Maybe that's what's so "astonishing!" "Johnny Mangano and His Astonishing Girlie! And Their Dog Kiki!"

> *She comes back and sits down at the make-up table and picks up KIKI's dress. She starts to sew it, then stops. She looks at herself in the mirror.*

You know, maybe I'm not such a wreck after all.
There are street walkers my age! Some are even older.
And they call themselves "dancers." I'm no more
worn out than they are! Look, you can die walking
the streets or you can die playing "girlie" to some
trained dogs . . . I'd rather die walking the streets . . .
At least I'd be my own leading lady . . . I'll just do
the same act I do now . . . minus the dogs! And
Johnny . . . Maybe I can do without Johnny too.

Pause.

I can, I can do without Johnny!

*KIKI barks. CARLOTTA jumps as if she'd been
stabbed in the back. Just then, JOHNNY enters.*

I'm leaving, Johnny.

JOHNNY:
What? You talking to yourself again?

CARLOTTA:
I said I'm leaving, Johnny! I just decided I'm going
to leave.

JOHNNY:
Don't be silly, Charlotte.

CARLOTTA:
I'm staying in Montréal, Johnny! I'm gonna go live
with my mother. And if I can't make it as a hooker,
I'll go to work in a pet shop.

JOHNNY:
What the hell? You gone off your rocker for good?

CARLOTTA:
Nope!

JOHNNY:
Do you know what you're saying?

CARLOTTA:
Of course I do.

JOHNNY:
But you love me!

CARLOTTA:
I know, but I'm leaving anyway. I quit.

JOHNNY:
Oh, come on, Charlotte, don't tell me that on account
of what happened, I mean, just because we fought a
little more than usual, doesn't mean you have to
make such a production? It wasn't serious! Come on,
I'm sorry . . . You know I love you, my gorgeous
Charlotte . . . Let's forget all about it . . . I'll get you
that new costume you wanted . . . What would I do
if you left, eh?

CARLOTTA:
You'll just keep on going.

JOHNNY:
Oh but, Sugar, you're a lot better with the dogs than
I am, you know that . . . And Kiki only listens to
you, you're the only one she likes!

CARLOTTA:
She can drop dead! Yes, goddamn it, she can drop
dead! I hate her! And I'm leaving!

> The STAGE MANAGER sticks his head in the
> door.

STAGE MANAGER:
Two minutes! Two minutes!

JOHNNY:
>Fuck off, you creep!

The STAGE MANAGER disappears.

>Now look, Charlotte, you know I need you. I've gotta have a girl!

CARLOTTA:
>Then go find another one! The States are full of "girlies." In fact, that's all they've got down there, nothing but "girlies!" But hell, take advantage of your stay in Montréal and try to find another sucker like me. You never know, you might be lucky twice.

JOHNNY: *grabbing her by the neck*
>You can't do this to me, my little sweetie pie. The show's gonna start any minute! There might be important people in the house!

CARLOTTA:
>I don't care, Johnny, I don't care! You hear me, I'm too happy, I don't care!

JOHNNY:
>You can't do this to me, you can't leave me alone, I can't do the act by myself.

CARLOTTA:
>Sure you can, Johnny . . .

>*The music for the beginning of the act can be heard.*

JOHNNY:
>Charlotte, it's time to go on.

CARLOTTA:
>Well, go on . . . Hurry up . . . Go get the dogs . . .

JOHNNY:
> I can't do it alone, Charlotte, I can't do it alone. You
> know that!

CARLOTTA:
> Of course you can, Johnny . . . Just tell yourself you
> can do it.

> *The STAGE MANAGER sticks his head in the*
> *door.*

STAGE MANAGER:
> You're on, Mister Mangano, you're on . . .

> *JOHNNY runs behind the screen, gets his tuxedo*
> *and grabs CHARLOTTE by the hand.*

JOHNNY:
> Come on, hurry, it's starting . . .

CARLOTTA: *softly smiling*
> I told you Johnny, I'm not going . . .

> *The STAGE MANAGER comes in.*

STAGE MANAGER:
> They're waiting for you on stage, Mister Managano . . .

M.C.:
> Le chic cabaret, "Coconut Inn," a l'honneur de vous
> présenter pour la première fois à Montréal, "Johnny
> Mangano and His Astonishing Dogs!"

> *A crescendo from the orchestra is heard.*
> *CARLOTTA shoves JOHNNY out the door.*

CARLOTTA:
> Well, hurry up, go on, it's starting . . .

The orchestra stops. Murmuring from the audience is heard. The five "Coconut Inn" DANCERS peer into the room.

JOHNNY:
Charlotte! Come on! It's started . . .

M.C.:
Le chic cabaret, "Coconut Inn," a l'honneur de vous présenter . . .

JOHNNY:
Charlotte!

M.C.:
For the first time, in our beautiful Montréal, the city of Expo '67 . . .

JOHNNY:
What am I gonna look like?

M.C.:
. . . a sensational number . . .

CARLOTTA:
Go on, Johnny, go on!

M.C.:
. . . "Johnny Mangano and His Astonishing Dogs!"

CARLOTTA:
For once in your life, show me you're a man! Take them out by yourself, your goddamned dogs.

Rustling from the audience is heard.

M.C.:
If they don't come out, we'll bring back the girls! Maybe one of the dogs has distemper. That reminds me of a little bitch named Marguerite, I used to know . . .

Laughter is heard. CARLOTTA puts her head in her hands. JOHNNY is leaning against the door sobbing.

JOHNNY:

I can't do it alone! You can't leave me like this. The guys are all in the audience! I'm gonna look like a fool. You don't want people to laugh at me, do you? And you, why do you want to do this to me? I know you're not that cruel, Charlotte. Don't you understand? I need you. You're right, right down the line! If you leave, I'm done for! I beg you . . . in front of everyone . . . to stay, Charlotte!

JOHNNY is at CARLOTTA's feet. CARLOTTA looks in the mirror and sees the tableau.

CARLOTTA:

He can't make it alone! He can't do it without me!

Pause.

Green. Okay, Carlotta, you'd better fix yourself up so you look pretty in green lights.

She takes KIKI's wedding dress and runs out of the room.

Come on, Kiki, we're late! Hurry it up, into the pretty pink lights! Mama will be right behind you, doing her stuff . . .

The orchestra launches into a South American number. Applause and whistling, are heard. JOHNNY runs out onto the stage.

Gloria Star

Backstage at the "Coconut Inn." In heading for the stage, CARLOTTA passes the FIVE DANCERS who were grouped around the dressing room door at the end of the previous scene.

CARLOTTA: *to the Girls*
> You came to watch the show, eh? To see a tough-minded woman in action? If it's lessons you want, come and see your Aunt Carlotta. She'll teach you all there is to know about how to keep your man.

MARGOT: *ironically*
> Oh! I beg your pardon!

LISE:
> Excuse us . . .

LAURETTE:
> Stand aside for Madame . . .

CARLOTTA stands beside the STAGE MANAGER waiting to make her entrance. She is holding Kiki, a dreadful pink poodle, in her arms. The STAGE MANAGER, a Frenchman with a very pronounced accent, is busy calling cues and giving orders to his ASSISTANT.

STAGE MANAGER:

Paul . . . Paul . . . The curtains aren't open enough . . . Try to pull them a bit . . . But be careful that no one sees you . . .

Speaking into his telephone.

Louis, can you hear me? Blue when the dog jumps through the circle . . . Blue! That's right. Now give me some green for the girl's entrance . . .

A crescendo from the orchestra is heard. The GIRLS have surrounded the STAGE MANAGER and CARLOTTA. The M.C. is with them.

M.C.:

What's going on back here?

STAGE MANAGER:

That's your cue, Madame.

CARLOTTA:

I know my cue, sweetie-pie, I've been doing it for twelve years. Oh God, the wedding dress! Oh well, I don't have time now!

Everyone laughs. CARLOTTA sticks the wedding dress in the STAGE MANAGER's hands and runs on stage, a triumphant smile on her face.

STAGE MANAGER:

Pink! Pink! That's it. Green spot on the girl.

M.C.:
What happened?

MARGOT: *to the STAGE MANAGER*
There's a dressing down for you!

LISE:
That'd make a nice hat.

MARGOT:
Oh yeah! You'd be real cute with it on.

> *She tries to place the hat on the STAGE MANAGER's head. He pulls it off with a huff and the GIRLS laugh.*

MARGOT:
Wow! This stuff isn't cheap. None of us could afford a costume like this.

STAGE MANAGER:
Don't worry. You'll never need a dress like that.

MARGOT:
I know, sweetheart, I'm not the kind they marry.

LISE:
Why not? Why won't you get married?

> *The others laugh.*

STAGE MANAGER: *speaking into his telephone*
Careful with the next one, you missed it yesterday . . .

LAURETTE: *looking onstage*
Maybe her boyfriend's sexy, but I wouldn't want to be stuck with those dogs.

STAGE MANAGER:
Try to get it right on with mine.

73

M.C.: *to MARGOT*
>You got a cigarette?

MARGOT:
>Is that all you can do, bum cigarettes?

M.C.:
>Oh, no, I can do lots of other things.

>*MARGOT bursts out laughing.*

MARGOT:
>I'd sure like to see that. It must be a riot.

DIANE: *to the STAGE MANAGER*
>Did I get a phone call? My boyfriend was supposed to call me . . .

LISE:
>Well, dogs or no dogs, I wouldn't kick him out of bed.

STAGE MANAGER:
>Yeah, yeah, I know it's hard with the dogs, but keep your eye on the pink poodle . . . Go!

>*He pushes some levers.*

>Good! Perfect! You see?

GIGI: *looking at the STAGE MANAGER*
>Well, he's not bad, but it takes more than that to make me faint . . .

LAURETTE: *indicating the STAGE MANAGER*
>Oh, sure, we know he's your type.

GIGI:
>And what's that supposed to mean?

M.C.: *imitating the STAGE MANAGER*
>Ladies! Ladies! They'll hear you out in the house.

STAGE MANAGER: *to the M.C.*
> Shhh! They'll hear you out in the house.

> *Everyone laughs.*

STAGE MANAGER: *speaking into his telephone*
> What? I can't hear you . . .

DIANE:
> Look, will somebody tell me . . .

LAURETTE:
> No, nobody phoned you. Christ! Why don't you call
> him? That's what you do every night anyway. And
> what's more, you never get him. He's always in some
> bar, plastered . . .

> *DIANE goes out.*

STAGE MANAGER:
> No, she didn't have time to put the wedding dress
> on . . . Hey, you should have seen the fireworks back
> here . . .

M.C.: *to MARGOT*
> What happened anyway?

GIGI: *to MARGOT*
> I don't know why you made me buy this bra. It cuts
> me like a knife.

MARGOT:
> You'll get used to it . . .

STAGE MANAGER:
> She wanted to quit the act . . . It was one hell of a . . .
> Watch it, blue!

M.C.: *to GIGI*
> You shouldn't wear one at all.

LAURETTE:

Aren't you funny. Mind your own business . . . Can't you just see us doing that with no bras? They'd be flying all over the place. You want a cigarette? Okay, but now go play in traffic, eh?

LISE:

Still, that must take a lot of patience . . . To teach 'em all that stuff . . .

DIANE comes back.

DIANE:

If he doesn't call, I'm gonna have a nervous breakdown.

LAURETTE:

Why don't you do that, then we can have some peace.

STAGE MANAGER:

Red!

GIGI:

She's still good looking though . . .

LAURETTE:

Sure, all she has to do is stand around behind the dogs. That's easy.

STAGE MANAGER:

Yes, thanks, she's much better . . . The doctor came . . . It's only the flu . . . How's your wife?

MARGOT:

Come on, girls. Time for a break. Let's go flop in the dressing room . . .

GIGI:

It's too hot . . .

LAURETTE:
> Sure, we know, you want to hang around your Prince
> Charming.

> *The others laugh.*

GIGI:
> Aren't you funny!

> *DIANE comes back again.*

DIANE:
> He's not there.

M.C.: *to GIGI*
> If it's too hot in your dressing room . . .

GIGI:
> I've got a feeling it'd be even hotter in yours.

MARGOT:
> Hey, for a beginner, you can sure take care of yourself
> . . . She shut you up, eh, creep?

> *They all laugh. A WOMAN walks in the midst
> of the laughter. She passes through the group
> and goes to the STAGE MANAGER.*

THE GIRLS:
> Hey . . . Watch it . . . What's going on? . . . Who's
> pushing? . . .

THE WOMAN: *to the STAGE MANAGER*
> Is everything ready? The star has arrived! She'll be
> out any minute.

MARGOT:
> My God! When she arrives, she arrives!

STAGE MANAGER: *who hasn't understood*
> The orchestra's late again? But, we rehearsed that bit the day before yesterday.

THE WOMAN:
> Young man!

STAGE MANAGER:
> What? It's the girl who's going too fast?

He laughs.

THE WOMAN:
> Young man, I'm talking to you!

The STAGE MANAGER jumps.

LAURETTE:
> Wow! Will you dig that!

MARGOT:
> Talk about having your master's voice!

STAGE MANAGER:
> What? What's the matter?

THE WOMAN:
> We've just arrived . . . The star of your show is here . . . Shes getting dressed.

STAGE MANAGER:
> Oh! So you're Gloria Star's agent?

LISE:
> An agent! A real agent!

STAGE MANAGER:
> We'd given up on you! Why didn't you get here for the first show? We didn't even have time for one rehearsal.

THE WOMAN:
>   Young man, I am not responsible for snowstorms that
>   close airports.

LAURETTE:
>   Oh, the plane couldn't land . . .

MARGOT:
>   What a shame . . . Poor things . . .

THE WOMAN:
>   Is everything ready?

STAGE MANAGER:
>   Yes, Ma'am, it's all ready . . .

GIGI:
>   Sure, we've been waiting for you like the Messiah!

THE WOMAN:
>   Because Madame Star is no amateur.

LAURETTE:
>   Wow! She lays it on, eh?

STAGE MANAGER: *speaking into his telephone*
>   Sorry, buddy . . . It's the star, she's just arrived.

MARGOT:
>   Star, my foot.

STAGE MANAGER:
>   The star! . . . Yes, the stripper . . . We're all set for
>   her act, aren't we? . . . Yeah, she goes on right after
>   the dogs.

LAURETTE:
>   And we went just before them . . .

THE WOMAN:
>   That's the stage . . .

LAURETTE: *murmuring*
>No, Madame, that's the dressing room! And the stage is downstairs, in the cellar.

THE WOMAN:
>I beg your pardon?

LAURETTE:
>Nothing, forget it . . . Alright, I'm going to withdraw into my apartments . . . I've got some wash to do . . . You coming, stars?

>*To the STAGE MANAGER.*

>See you later, young man . . .

>*The FIVE GIRLS walk off laughing. Haughtily, THE WOMAN watches them go.*

THE WOMAN:
>Birdbrains!

STAGE MANAGER:
>The next one's pink . . . And I give her the juice when the monkey jumps out of the box . . . Go!

>*Loud laughter from the audience is heard, then applause and whistling. THE WOMAN casts her eyes towards heaven. The STAGE MANAGER grabs the GOPHER as he goes by.*

STAGE MANAGER:
>Paul! Paul! Could you see to it that the orchestra knows that Gloria Star . . .

GOPHER:
>Who?

STAGE MANAGER:
>Gloria Star! The star! She's here. Tell the piano player. But don't scream it in his ear, you know?

The STAGE MANAGER becomes aware that
THE WOMAN is standing behind him.

STAGE MANAGER:
Are you watching the show?

THE WOMAN:
Trained dog numbers have never been my passion,
I'm afraid . . .

STAGE MANAGER:
If you're trying to . . . Blue! If you're trying to judge
the stage, you needn't worry about a thing. It'll all
go smooth as glass. Madame Star can rest assured that
we . . .

THE WOMAN:
Gloria Star never worries, young man! Gloria Star
could do her act without music, without lights, in
the street, and still be sublime!

The STAGE MANAGER holds back a laugh.

STAGE MANAGER:
Madame Star won't have to do her act without music,
lights, or out in the street. We're ready.

THE WOMAN:
Do you think so?

STAGE MANAGER: *turning toward her*
We are not a second rate house, lady. We are always
ready to face any problem. Especially the one of stars
arriving late.

THE WOMAN: *laughing*
Well, you see . . . This is Madame Star's first
appearance here, is it not?

STAGE MANAGER:
Yes, it's the first time . . . Pink!

THE WOMAN:
>Something tells me you don't know what's in store
>for you . . . Which reminds me, have all the clauses
>in the contract been respected? Is the shower of
>phosphorescent feathers ready?

STAGE MANAGER:
>Yes, Ma'am, the shower of phosporescent feathers is
>ready.

THE WOMAN:
>Gloria Star will not perform without her phosphores-
>cent feathers, you know? Gloria Star is the only artist
>to use them and her reputation . . .

STAGE MANAGER:
>You just said a minute ago that Madame Star could
>do her act without music, lights, and out in the
>street. But not without her feathers?

THE WOMAN:
>Is the music ready too? You did receive the music,
>didn't you?

STAGE MANAGER:
>Red! No, sorry, blue. Yes, Ma'am, I told you already,
>EVERYTHING is ready. You'll have your feathers,
>your original music, your standing ovations from a
>delirious audience, everything. Would you like the
>Ride of the Walkyries as well? And a symphony
>orchestra? Would you like to have the Vietnam war
>brought to Montréal for background sound? Orange!
>You seem to forget that it was also in your contract
>that Madame Star was to arrive three hours prior to
>the first show, not five minutes before the second
>one.

>*Speaking into his telephone.*

>Listen, I'm having a fight with Gloria Star's agent,
>I can't do two things at once.

82

THE WOMAN:

> I take it that you are the genius responsible for lights
> in this establishment. Try to measure up, my boy.
> You must always try to measure up to the standards
> of Gloria Star . . .

STAGE MANAGER:

> Look, I've seen enough stripppers since I've been
> here . . .

THE WOMAN:

> Gloria Star is no ordinary stripper! Gloria Star is the
> greatest stripper! Gloria Star is an asteroid glimmering
> in the galaxy of strippers.

STAGE MANAGER:

> Yeah, they all say that . . .

THE WOMAN grabs him by the wrist.

THE WOMAN:

> If I tell you that Gloria Star is the greatest stripper,
> then she is the greatest stripper, understand? No one
> in the world of show business has attained the
> perfection of Gloria Star. Never! I spent five years
> building Gloria Star, making her a celebration of
> beauty. And I succeeded. So get it through your
> head, young man, the show you're going to see
> tonight is unique in it's genre. I've spent my life
> planning it; I've spent my life in search of the perfect
> body and when I found it, I put every ounce of my
> experience and love into this apotheosis, this ultimate
> creation of beauty in all its splendour. Everything
> I couldn't do myself when I was young because I
> had no one to guide me, and perhaps because I
> didn't have the talent, I have done for her! She is
> the crowning glory of my life . . . And now I want
> to create something even bigger, something that
> has never been seen . . . But I can't find . . .

STAGE MANAGER: *not listening anymore*
Okay, okay, she's the greatest . . . fine by me. Now, would you mind letting me work? I don't have a strip show to prepare, but if you want your lights to be right . . .

Something seems to have struck THE WOMAN. She stares at THE STAGE MANAGER.

I know it's my job to call the cues, but . . . Okay . . . okay . . . Hold on . . . The next one is orange . . .

THE WOMAN: *with a vision*
A man . . .

STAGE MANAGER:
Okay . . . Go!

Everything turns amber.

THE WOMAN:
Tell me, young man . . .

STAGE MANAGER:
Lady, I'm working and you're bothering me, can't you understand that?

He returns to his lighting board.

THE WOMAN:
I wanted to ask you . . . I look at you and . . . Have you ever thought about . . . about performing on stage?

STAGE MANAGER:
Who? Me? . . . On stage?

THE WOMAN:
I mean . . . Have you ever thought of . . . I don't know, becoming an actor or a singer? . . . Or a dancer? . . .

STAGE MANAGER:
No, I've never thought of any of that!

THE WOMAN:
Ah, but have you never thought of glory?

STAGE MANAGER:
No, really, now you're going a bit far. No, lady, I've
never thought of glory. Do I look like someone who'd
even dream of glory? I'm just a waiter, lady, and I
do the lights when they need me. This week we've
got some colour freaks with neon dogs and a stripper
who does her act with a shower of phosphorescent
feathers, so they asked me to just do the lights.
That's all.

*The STAGE MANAGER returns angrily to his
work. THE WOMAN comes up very close to him.*

THE WOMAN:
And what if I offered you glory?

STAGE MANAGER:
What? What did you say?

THE WOMAN:
What if I offered you glory?

STAGE MANAGER:
Just what would you like me to do with it?

THE WOMAN:
Do you think you're funny? Or are you completely
stupid? Do you even know what it means? . . .

STAGE MANAGER:
Glory?

THE WOMAN:
Glory!

STAGE MANAGER:

Yes, lady, I know what it means, lady, but I'm not interested, lady. Besides, how would you go about offering me glory?

THE WOMAN:

Have you ever thought what would happen if one day a man were to undress on stage?

STAGE MANAGER:

What! A man! You're out of your mind! A man! Nude on stage? Please, this has gone on long enough! Go get your glory dressed and let me do my work.

She grabs him by the wrist.

THE WOMAN:

I'm not joking! The era of woman-as-object is over, my friend. We are beginning the era of man-as-object.

STAGE MANAGER:

She's crazy! I think I'll keep my clothes on, lady.

A crescendo from the orchestra is heard, then laughter and applause. The STAGE MANAGER goes back to his lighting board.

THE WOMAN:

Look at that ridiculous woman out there . . . Fifteen years ago I might have been able to do something with her . . . A big star! But today it's too late! It's too late for her . . . and for me. I have produced the most perfect act in its genre, young man. Gloria Star! I can do no better! Now I must look elsewhere.

STAGE MANAGER:

Why don't you do just that! Green!

THE WOMAN:

I offer you glory! If you refuse, you'll make me force your hand. Think of all those who dream of glory their entire lives without ever being able to attain it. I offer you the greatest innovation of the twentieth century!

STAGE MANAGER:
Why me?

THE WOMAN:
Why not you?

STAGE MANAGER:
The world is full of ballet dancers who couldn't ask for more . . .

THE WOMAN:
No, I need someone like you . . .

STAGE MANAGER:
Oh, I get it . . . Look, if that's how you make a play for a guy . . .

THE WOMAN:
I'm not making a play for you!

She takes his telephone away.

And put down that ridiculous thing when I talk to you. Look at me! Look at me! For twenty-five years I have produced the most successful shows in the world because I have always given the public what it wants . . . and even a bit more. The greatest dancers, the greatest strippers have been in my hands, and they have known what Gloria Star knows today. Glory! And it's thanks to their bodies. The human body is the masterpiece of creation. The whole of antiquity lavished praise on the human body. Look at the Greeks. I've spent my life showing masterpieces to the public. I've spent my life proving to the world, through my art, that the human body is the most beautiful thing there is. But there's a part of the public I've always neglected, a part of the public that is about to come of age. It's that part of the public that is demanding something new! Young man, women also want to be provoked and transported.

STAGE MANAGER:
Lady! You're really off your rocker, and I beg you to please return to your star's dressing room before I have to drag you there myself!

THE WOMAN:
How exciting! Imagine, a group of women who are . . .

STAGE MANAGER:
Shut up!

Speaking into his telephone.

I've got a raving lunatic on my hands down here! She is offering me a job as a stripper . . . Yeah, that's right, striptease . . . No, not in drag . . . As a man! Completely naked! On a stage!

THE WOMAN:
I see a large open space . . . The orchestra playing some savage piece . . .

STAGE MANAGER:
Red! Can't you just see it? My wife would love it!

THE WOMAN:
Lights of all colours explode on the scene and you appear, dressed . . . dressed . . . Right, here we'd have a little problem of clothes . . .

STAGE MANAGER:
Spot on the dog . . . Pink! I'll do the blue.

THE WOMAN:
We'll work that out . . . Yes, we'll work it out so that you won't have too much trouble taking off your clothes . . . I mean, pants . . . you know . . . Ah! I've

got it. You'll appear dressed as an Arab. The Sheik of Arabie! With your whole train. The spectacle of spectacles! I'm offering you a huge show. With an entire harem. You would appear dressed as an Arab in the midst of your women, your slaves and your animals. Superb women, thinly veiled, shiny black slaves and . . . and camels! And slowly you begin to undress . . . You take off your burnous, your caftan, you unlace your sandals before an audience of delirious women!

STAGE MANAGER:

Red! Everything in red! That's all, just red! For the finale.

THE WOMAN:

You're not listening to me! The women are crawling at your feet. I'm offering you collective hysteria.

STAGE MANAGER: *laughing*

That's it for the dogs, now let's get ready for the strip! I'm working, lady! But don't stop, I'm listening with one ear. You're hilarious. You sure you're not the act? Gloria Star isn't a comic, is she?

THE WOMAN:

Ha! You laugh at me! That's a challenge! That's good! I'll convince you! Whether you want it or not, young man, you're going to have glory! Take my word for it!

Suddenly, she moves away. A crescendo from the orchestra is heard, then applause.

M.C.:

Here they are, ladies and gentlemen! Aren't they gorgeous? Et voilà, mesdames et messieurs, ne sont-ils pas gorgeux? Come on, une bonne main d'applaudisse-ments! A good hand for our stars, ladies and gentlemen! Johnny Mangano and His Astonishing Dogs! Johnny Mangano et Ses Etonnants Chiens! Thank you, Johnny, you are the most! Vous l'avez, l'affaire, continuez! Isn't that right, folks, aren't they the greatest?

Weak applause.

C'est ça . . . They're tops . . .

JOHNNY and CARLOTTA bow and run offstage.

JOHNNY:
> You did it on purpose to make her fall! I saw you! You did it on purpose!

CARLOTTA:
> Come on, Johnny! As if I'd start making the dogs fall now!

JOHNNY:
> And you didn't even put Kiki in her wedding dress.

CARLOTTA:
> Look, Johnny, I couldn't watch you bawling and put Kiki's dress on at the same time!

She slams the dressing room door.

M.C.:
> And now, ladies and gentlemen, the moment you've all been waiting for. Le grand moment de la soirée . . . The star of our show. Ladies and gentlemen, I give you Gloria Star!

STAGE MANAGER:
> Blackout!

Blackout.

Lights!

When the lights come back up, the set has completely disappeared. There is no one left but the STAGE MANAGER, BERTHE, CARLOTTA, JOHNNY and THE WOMAN, standing in a big empty studio.

Suddenly, out of the darkness there appears an extraordinarily beautiful DANCER. Striptease music begins. The DANCER starts her act. The STAGE MANAGER seems hypnotized. Little by little, the DANCER's act becomes a kind of ritual combining dance steps with slow, disquieting gestures.

THE WOMAN begins to laugh loudly. The DANCER goes toward CARLOTTA and with a flick of her hand makes her disappear. The same with BERTHE. The DANCER turns toward the STAGE MANAGER, gesturing for him to follow her. He goes towards her dancing.

THE WOMAN laughs more and more loudly.

DOORMAN:
Showtime! Showtime!

Surprise, Surprise

Three women are installed in front of three telephones.

LAURETTE is in the midst of a "lively" conversation.

LAURETTE:
> I don't care what you say, let kids get away with that nonsense and they're out of hand in no time. No kidding.

> *Pause.*

> No kidding!

> *Pause.*

> No kidding! Well, I never!

> *JEANNINE dials LAURETTE's number.*

JEANNINE:
> I'm getting sick of this.

LAURETTE:
Look, you've gotta use psychology.

JEANNINE:
Still busy! She's gonna drop dead from exhaustion!

She hangs up.

LAURETTE:
If it was me, I'd have straightened him out long ago!

JEANNINE:
I'll give it one more try . . .

LAURETTE:
Too strict! Listen, you're never too strict with boys!

JEANNINE: *dialing LAURETTE's number*
If she's still talking, I swear I'll take the bus over to her place and strangle her with her own telephone. telephone.

LAURETTE:
I've never let a child step on my toes!

JEANNINE:
She's still talking.

She hangs up.

LAURETTE:
It's a good thing I never had any, eh, 'cause they'd have been drilled like soldiers!

JEANNINE:
Enough is enough, I'm gonna call the operator. She's probably died with the phone in her hands.

She dials "O."

LAURETTE:

> I mean, look at my sister's boy . . . Er . . . Now that's
> silly, I've forgotten his name . . . Oh, for Godsakes . . .
> Isn't that crazy, he's my own nephew! Gilbert! That's
> it! Well, when Gilbert comes here, he sits in his chair
> and he doesn't budge! He was a real brat too! I took
> care of him alright.

JEANNINE:

> Sounds like the operator's on vacation. Hello? Oh, er
> . . . Yes, hello. I phoned because I've been trying to
> reach my girlfriend for the last . . . I don't know,
> hour-and-a-half, but it keeps ringing busy, so I was
> wondering if she isn't dead or something . . . I mean
> sick . . . or you know, maybe she just forgot to put
> her phone back on the hook . . .

LAURETTE:

> It's good for them, every now and then a smack in
> the face . . .

JEANNINE:

> Could you try it for me?

LAURETTE:

> Or a well placed whack with the strap. That never did
> any harm.

JEANNINE:

> The number? Oh! Oh, her number. I beg your pardon!

LAURETTE:

> I know this isn't the nineteenth century, but I didn't
> say to kill him, did I? Besides, maybe we oughta be
> in the nineteenth century, 'cause kids have gotten
> soft. Suffering has to be learned like everything else
> . . . Hello? What's that? You still there? What was
> that funny noise?

JEANNINE:

> She is on the phone, eh? You couldn't ask her to hang up, could you?

LAURETTE:

> I thought we'd been cut off . . .

JEANNINE:

> It's very, very important!

LAURETTE:

> You ever try to hang up on me, dear, you'll live to regret it!

JEANNINE:

> You haven't the right to do that, eh? . . . Well, thanks anyway . . . At least I know she isn't dead . . .

LAURETTE:

> What? Someone's trying to get through? How do you know? It's the operator who does that? That means they listen to us! Whenever they want!

> *Whispering.*

> You think she's listening now?

JEANNINE:

> Boy, an hour-and-a-half! I hope she isn't talking to her sister who's a nun in the Congo!

LAURETTE:

> So they can spy on us and there's nothing we can do? Hey you, the spies, if you're listening in, I hope you know you've got a dirty job!

JEANNINE:

> Another hour-and-a-half and I'll be too late!

LAURETTE:

> Anyway, I've gotta hang up, my hand's fallen asleep . . .

JEANNINE:

Her phone's gonna melt in her ear!

LAURETTE:

And I don't like to talk with people snooping around. Yeah, okay, I'll call you tomorrow. Bye! You can hang up now, nosey!

She hangs up.

JEANNINE:

Now, do I try it again or do I get on the bus and go yank out her vocal chords?

LAURETTE:

Oh, my God, it's two-thirty! Jeannine was gonna phone me at one!

JEANNINE:

I'll try it one last time!

They both dial at the same time.

LAURETTE:

What's going on?

JEANNINE:

I don't believe it. She's been talking so long they've cut her off. Hello?

LAURETTE:

Hello? Jeannine?

JEANNINE:

Is that you, Laurette? How did you get on the line?

LAURETTE:

I just phoned you!

JEANNINE:

> I just phoned you, but it didn't ring. You through talking to your sister in the Congo?

LAURETTE:

> What?

JEANNINE:

> Forget it . . . I've been trying to get you for an hour-and-a-half!

LAURETTE:

> Yeah, I'm awful sorry, I just remembered you were gonna call. I was talking to my sister-in-law, Aline. You know what a gossip she is!

JEANNINE:

> The one who's deaf and dumb?

LAURETTE:

> No, not Ali-ce, Ali-ne!

JEANNINE:

> I was worried.

> *Laughing.*

> What a joke that'd be, eh? This girl who spends two hours a day on the phone with her deaf and dumb sister-in-law, just so she can hog the whole conversation.

LAURETTE:

> Okay, that'll do! What did you decide about Madeleine?

JEANNINE:

> Aren't you funny! "What did I decide!" We decided it together! I've already phoned everyone else, you're the only one I couldn't get hold of. It's all set, we're giving Madeleine a surprise party.

LAURETTE:
>
> Today?

JEANNINE:
>
> Well, today's her birthday. We're not going to wait till Easter!

LAURETTE:
>
> That's not what I mean. Can't we wait till the weekend? That'd give us time to get ready.

JEANNINE:
>
> No, no, if we don't do it today, it doesn't count . . . And we've made it for suppertime 'cause the girls like to go to bed early . . .

LAURETTE:
>
> Aw, that's no fun! That means we all go to bed at ten o'clock again!

> *MADELEINE dials LAURETTE's number.*

MADELEINE:
>
> My finger's going to fall off just dialing this stupid number!

JEANNINE:
>
> Madeleine herself likes to go to bed early and it's her party, for Godsake.

MADELEINE:
>
> It's still busy!

> *She hangs up.*

JEANNINE:
>
> She doesn't live far from you, so why don't you pick her up . . . Give her a call later on.

LAURETTE:
>
> What am I gonna tell her?

JEANNINE:

What do you mean, what are you gonna tell her?

LAURETTE:

Does she know we're giving her a surprise party?

JEANNINE:

If she knew that, it wouldn't be much of a surprise, would it? All I told her was that we'd go out for supper together.

LAURETTE:

Well, for Godsake, if she doesn't know I'm coming, how do I tell her I'm gonna pick her up?

JEANNINE:

I don't know, invite yourself along. You can think of something. You're always telling everyone else what to do, but you never know what to do yourself.

LAURETTE:

What about the present? What do we do about that?

JEANNINE: *changing her tone*

Well, that's why I wanted to get a hold of you so bad . . . Can your husband still give us a deal?

LAURETTE:

What, again? Look, my husband's a jeweller. He's not Santa Claus!

JEANNINE:

No one's asking him to give us anything . . . we can pay, you know . . . A little gold chain or something, that shouldn't be too expensive, eh?

LAURETTE:

Gold *plated*?

JEANNINE:

Yeah . . .

LAURETTE:

> Come to think of it, there is one that's been lying around the window for ages . . . It's ugly as sin, but then, knowing Madeleine's taste . . .

MADELEINE:

> I'm gonna try to get Jeannine.

> *She dials the number.*

JEANNINE:

> Okay, but you don't have to make it some piece of junk, eh? What do you think, can your husband have it ready by five?

MADELEINE:

> Her too? Good God!

LAURETTE:

> If he can't, I'll go wrap it myself . . .

JEANNINE:

> This time, don't forget the price tag, eh, like you did with my bracelet? It wasn't the present that surprised me, it was the price. It must have cost you at least a quarter each!

LAURETTE:

> By the way, how much do you want to spend?

JEANNINE:

> As little as possible . . .

LAURETTE:

> A dollar per girl?

JEANNINE:

> I guess.

LAURETTE:

> How many are we, eight?

JEANNINE:
>   Seven.

LAURETTE:
>   Well, compared to that, dear, your present was bought by the Queen! Alright, enough of this. I've got to get off and run over to the shop.

JEANNINE:
>   Okay. Five o'clock at the Mont-Royal Bar B-Q . . .

LAURETTE:
>   I'll be there.

JEANNINE:
>   Alright, see you later.

LAURETTE:
>   Bye-bye.

>   *They hang up.*

>   *MADELEINE dials LAURETTE's number.*

I wonder if it's a good idea, having the party at the Mont-Royal Bar B-Q?

>   *LAURETTE's phone rings.*

MADELEINE:
>   Finally!

LAURETTE:
>   That'll be Jeannine phoning me back. I'll see what she thinks . . .

>   *She picks up the receiver.*

Hey, Jeannine, you sure it's a good idea to take Madeleine to the Mont-Royal for a surprise party?

Won't she know what's going on? I mean, we always
go there.

MADELEINE:
What? Hello?

LAURETTE:
Hello? Jeannine?

MADELEINE:
Er . . . no . . . no, excuse me, I must have the wrong
number.

She hangs up.

LAURETTE:
Oh God, that was Madeleine!

MADELEINE:
A surprise party? What's she talking about?

LAURETTE:
I've got to call Jeannine.

MADELEINE:
Is this my birthday? It's my birthday and I don't even
know it?

The phone rings at JEANNINE's.

JEANNINE:
Hello?

LAURETTE:
Jeannine?

JEANNINE:
Ah, Laurette, I was just gonna phone you back . . .

MADELEINE:
What day is this?

JEANNINE:

Listen, do you think it's a good idea to take Madeleine to the Mont-Royal?

MADELEINE:

My God, what month is this?

JEANNINE:

Won't she know what's up if we say we're going there?

MADELEINE:

I'm all confused!

LAURETTE:

Will you let me talk? I can't get two words in.

JEANNINE:

Aren't you in a snit?

MADELEINE:

For Godsake, when's my birthday?

LAURETTE:

I just made a terrible mistake!

JEANNINE:

Another one? How many's that today?

MADELEINE:

The . . . the 21st of February! My birthday is on the 21st of February!

LAURETTE:

Will you let me finish!

MADELEINE:

What month is this?

JEANNINE:

Well, talk!

MADELEINE:
There's snow outside, so at least it's winter.

LAURETTE:
Madeleine just called, and I thought it was you calling back, and I told her everything.

MADELEINE:
I'll phone the operator . . .

JEANNINE:
Oh, smart . . .

MADELEINE:
This is crazy, I'm so upset I don't know what day it is!

JEANNINE:
Brilliant!

LAURETTE:
But that's not the real mistake.

JEANNINE:
You mean it's worse than that?

MADELEINE:
Hello, operator, what day is this please?

LAURETTE:
It . . . It wasn't Madeleine that phoned.

JEANNINE:
What?

MADELEINE:
I know it's Monday, operator, I've got about two miles of laundry hanging out in the back.

JEANNINE:
You just told me it was her! Make up your mind!

MADELEINE:
>   I mean, what's the date?

LAURETTE:
>   I'm so upset I can't think straight. I mean, it wasn't
>   the real Madeleine who phoned.

MADELEINE:
>   What do you mean, you're not supposed to give that
>   information? What good are you anyway?

>   *She hangs up and dials another number.*

LAURETTE:
>   It was Madeleine Michaud who phoned.

JEANNINE:
>   So?

LAURETTE:
>   But it's Madeleine Simard who's having a birthday!
>   And when I mentioned the surprise party, Madeleine
>   Michaud pretended she had the wrong number.

JEANNINE:
>   So?

MADELEINE:
>   Hello? Police?

LAURETTE:
>   That means she'll think the surprise party is for her.

MADELEINE:
>   What day is this please?

JEANNINE:
>   What are you talking about? It's no where near her
>   birthday.

MADELEINE:

I know it's Monday. The date, dammit, the date?

LAURETTE:

Yes, but does she know it isn't her birthday? Did you invite her to the surprise party?

JEANNINE:

Which one do you mean?

LAURETTE:

Her. Madeleine Michaud, the one who's not having a birthday.

MADELEINE:

January 19th?

JEANNINE:

Lord, no, I forgot her. Well, anyway, she wasn't on my list.

MADELEINE:

So it's nowhere near my birthday.

LAURETTE:

So that's even worse. She's gonna think we're cooking up a big bash for her and that we'll pick her up at the last minute.

MADELEINE:

No, never mind, I don't need the time.

LAURETTE:

What are we gonna do?

MADELEINE:

I'm not crazy, you know!

She hangs up.

JEANNINE:

> We'll say the party's for her too.

LAURETTE:

> Are you crazy?

JEANNINE:

> What else can we do?

MADELEINE:

> They've prepared this big party for me and it isn't even my birthday. What am I gonna do?

JEANNINE:

> You want to phone her back and tell her you made a mistake? You want to tell her it was very stupid of you, but that we'll make it all up to her when it really is her birthday? Eh?

LAURETTE:

> Not on your life!

MADELEINE:

> For the love of God, what am I gonna do?

LAURETTE:

> I could never tell her that! She wasn't even invited.

MADELEINE:

> I'm gonna phone Laurette back and tell her she's made a mistake, that's all there is to it.

> *She dials LAURETTE's number.*

JEANNINE:

> Then there's no other choice but to have the party and pretend we think it's her birthday. By the way, when is her birthday?

MADELEINE:

Busy! They're all on the phone setting up my party!
Boy, oh boy!

LAURETTE:

I don't know . . . June?

JEANNINE:

Well, we're not far off, eh? . . . Alright, look, let's
phone her, 'cause if we leave it like this she'll be
waiting all night for someone to pick her up. And
she's crazy enough to think we'd forgotten her on the
day of her birthday.

LAURETTE:

Yeah, well it's not me who's gonna call her up and
invite her to a party that she thinks is for her, but
that's really for somebody else.

JEANNINE:

No, I can see it now, I'm the one who'll be stuck
with that.

MADELEINE:

But I can't do that. It'll spoil all their fun.

LAURETTE:

What about the other Madeleine?

JEANNINE:

What about her?

LAURETTE:

Don't we have a party for her?

JEANNINE:

Of course, we'll have the party for both of them.

LAURETTE:

That means two presents.

JEANNINE:
> Oh, I forgot about that!

LAURETTE:
> Another gold chain?

JEANNINE:
> I guess . . .

LAURETTE:
> Matching?

JEANNINE:
> Come on, they're not twins.

MADELEINE:
> But . . . how am I gonna act? Surprised, even though Laurette spilled the beans? But then, maybe she didn't recognize me? . . .

LAURETTE:
> Two bucks per girl?

JEANNINE:
> What can you do?

MADELEINE:
> Should I finally admit that it isn't my birthday, or do I let them keep thinking it is?

LAURETTE:
> Okay, I'll call the others. You phone and invite her . . .

JEANNINE:
> Oh, I hate this! Boy, do I hate this! Why didn't you keep your big mouth shut?

MADELEINE:
> Either way, it's not gonna work. They'll find out sooner or later, then I'm gonna look like a liar.

LAURETTE:
>It's not my fault.

JEANNINE:
>I always have to clean up your mess!

MADELEINE:
>Maybe I should wait till the party's over, then tell them. I can just see myself giving them back the present.

LAURETTE:
>Hey, I just thought of something else . . .

JEANNINE:
>What now?

LAURETTE:
>The cake!

MADELEINE:
>They'll all be mad at me again!

JEANNINE:
>Oh . . . We don't have time to worry about that . . . we'll just tell them to put tons of candles on it and the two Madeleines can blow them out together.

LAURETTE:
>At least we have to tell them to put an "s" on the end of "Happy Birthday, Madeleine."

JEANNINE:
>"Madeleine" never takes an "s."

LAURETTE:
>No?

JEANNINE:
>No.

LAURETTE:
Are you sure?

JEANNINE:
Laurette, it's a rule of grammar.

LAURETTE:
In grammar they say that "Madeleine" can't take an "s?"

JEANNINE:
No dear, they say that proper names don't take an "s." Just watch "Les Walton" on television, you'll see. It's only in English that it takes an "s."

LAURETTE:
Oh, I never noticed. Of course I don't watch that stuff anyway. But that's gonna look cheap, only one cake.

JEANNINE:
So, it'll look cheap, too bad! I'm not about to start baking cakes 'cause you stuck your foot in your mouth! Christ!

LAURETTE:
Don't get mad!

MADELEINE:
But I can't understand it, they didn't even invite me to my own party.

LAURETTE:
Alright, you phone her and I'll explain it to the others . . . Bye!

JEANNINE:
Okay, bye!

MADELEINE:
If one of them phones me now, I'll die on the spot.

112

JEANNINE: *looking in her address book*
>Muster up your courage, dear, and phone the false
>birthday girl.

>*She dials MADELEINE's number.*

MADELEINE:
>I'm too scared, I'm taking the phone off the hook.

>*She takes the receiver off the hook.*

JEANNINE:
>Another one who's tied herself to the phone. Maybe
>I'll get lucky and she'll hang herself with it. That'd
>take care of everything.

>*She hangs up.*

MADELEINE:
>But that's not very nice of me, they've gone to so
>much trouble . . . It's really very sweet of them.

>*She hangs up.*

LAURETTE:
>I'll start with Madeleine Simard . . . I have to tell her
>that I'll come and pick her up . . . Madeleine . . . I've
>gotta find a way to invite myself . . . Madeleine . . .
>Ah, here it is. Now no mistakes, eh, at least we want
>her to be surprised!

>*She dials the number.*

>*The phone rings, but it's the wrong MADELEINE.*

MADELEINE:
>It's them.

JEANNINE:
>I'll try it again . . .

She dials MADELEINE's number.

MADELEINE:
Hello?

LAURETTE:
Hello, Madeleine?

MADELEINE:
Er . . . yes . . .

JEANNINE:
Damn!

She hangs up.

LAURETTE:
This is Laurette . . . Listen, Jeannine just called me
and she tells me that you're going out for supper
together so I thought maybe I'd join you, you know
. . . Is that okay with you? . . . We haven't seen each
other for a long time, eh? . . . I'll come and pick you
up, so look for me around five-thirty, okay?

MADELEINE:
Er . . . okay.

LAURETTE:
Alright-y, see you later.

She hangs up.

JEANNINE dials MADELEINE's number again.

MADELEINE:
She must be crazy. I haven't talked to Jeannine.

The phone rings.

JEANNINE:
Don't tell me!

LAURETTE: *looking in her address book*
> Oh no! It can't be! I had the wrong number! I phoned the wrong Madeleine again!

MADELEINE:
> Hello?

JEANNINE:
> Hello, Madeleine? It's Jeannine . . . How are you doing? . . .

MADELEINE:
> Oh, I'm doing okay . . . You know how it is, some days you're not too sure . . .

JEANNINE:
> What are you doing tonight?

MADELEINE:
> Well . . . nothing special . . . I guess.

JEANNINE:
> You want to go out for supper to the Mont-Royal Bar B-Q? There's a whole bunch of us going . . .

LAURETTE dials a number.

Silence between JEANNINE and MADELEINE.

LAURETTE:
> Hello, Georgette? Guess what? . . .

JEANNINE:
> You still there?

MADELEINE:
> Yeah . . . Who's gonna be there?

JEANNINE:
> The usual gang . . . Why, don't you feel like it?

MADELEINE:
>Oh . . . yeah . . .

JEANNINE:
>Okay, well you're not far from me, so I'll stop and pick you up around five-thirty, okay?

MADELEINE:
>Well . . .

JEANNINE:
>See you then . . . bye!

>*She hangs up.*

MADELEINE:
>That's great, now they're both coming to get me.

JEANNINE:
>We'll still be talking about this ten years from now.

LAURETTE: *dramatically*
>Oh my God! You've gotta be kidding! What are we gonna do? I've got to phone Jeannine right away. Bye!

>*She hangs up and dials JEANNINE's number.*

MADELEINE:
>January 19th, January 19th . . . That rings a bell somehow . . .

JEANNINE:
>Again! That'll be Laurette thinking she's phoned Georgette! Hello?

LAURETTE:
>Is that you, Jeannine?

JEANNINE:
>No, it's Madeleine.

LAURETTE:
>
> What?

JEANNINE:
>
> You've made another mistake!

LAURETTE:
>
> Huh?

JEANNINE:
>
> No, I'm only kidding.

LAURETTE:
>
> This isn't the time! Wait till you hear what Georgette just told me!

JEANNINE:
>
> What is it this time?

LAURETTE:
>
> Madeleine Michaud and Madeleine Simard haven't been talking to one another for two weeks! Madeleine Simard ran off with Madeleine Michaud's boyfriend!

JEANNINE:
>
> Oh, brother!

LAURETTE:
>
> So there's no way we can invite them to the same party!

MADELEINE:
>
> January 19th, that's that pig, Madeleine Simard's birthday!

LAURETTE:
>
> Let alone blow out the same candles on the same cake!

JEANNINE:
>
> What are we gonna do?

MADELEINE:
>   I'm not going there tonight! Oh no!

JEANNINE:
>   Have you got a gun?

MADELEINE:
>   Not on your bloody life!

LAURETTE:
>   A gun? What for?

JEANNINE:
>   So you can blow your brains out, then clean up your
>   own mess!

>   *She hangs up.*

MADELEINE:
>   They're doing this to make a fool of me, the bitches!
>   Wait till I phone them back, I'll tell them what to
>   do with their party!

>   *She dials LAURETTE's number.*

LAURETTE:
>   What is she, crazy?

JEANNINE:
>   She's crazy enough to take me seriously!

>   *She also dials LAURETTE's number.*

>   *LAURETTE's phone rings.*

LAURETTE:
>   I feel another disaster coming on. Hello?

MADELEINE:
>   Laurette! It's Madeleine! Madeleine Michaud!

JEANNINE:

Oh my God, she's still on the line!

LAURETTE:

I was right, it's another disaster!

MADELEINE:

What's all this about a party?

LAURETTE:

Er . . .

MADELEINE:

It was your idea, wasn't it?

LAURETTE:

Er, no, no . . .

MADELEINE:

Then it was hers, that cow, Madeleine Simard. You want to humiliate me, eh? Isn't that it? I suppose the whole gang heard the news and you were all delighted I lost my boyfriend, eh? Well, I won't be laughed at that easily, you'll see!

LAURETTE:

Madeleine, listen!

MADELIENE:

Don't try to get out of it! You want a surprise party, you'll get one! I'm going there tonight. And don't bother to pick me up, I'll get there on my own! But the rest of you better watch out, eh? If you've never seen a birthday cake go flying through the air and a fifty year old birthday girl take off after it, then prepare yourselves for a treat!

She hangs up.

119

LAURETTE:

Oh my God! And she'll do it too! Right in the middle of the Mont-Royal Bar B-Q! I've gotta warn Jeannine.

MADELEINE:

Now the other one! She'll get a piece of my mind too.

The two women dial JEANNINE's number.

Her phone rings.

JEANNINE:
Now what? Hello?

MADELEINE:
Damn!

She hangs up.

LAURETTE:

Hello, Jeannine! We can't have a party! We've gotta stop the whole thing! We've gotta cancel everything!

JEANNINE:
What?

LAURETTE:

Madeleine Michaud just phoned. She wants to kill us all! She wants to come to the Mont-Royal and smash everything! She thinks we did this on purpose to make her look stupid. What are we gonna do? Say something, Jeannine!

JEANNINE:

Someday we'll be laughing about this, but right now, it ain't funny!

MADELEINE:

And as for Madeleine Simard, she'll find out what I think of her.

JEANNINE:
Look, there's only one thing to do. We've gotta change restaurants.

MADELEINE:
The dirty boyfriend thief!

LAURETTE:
What do you mean, change restaurants?

MADELEINE:
I'll pull her hair out, one by one. No, in handfulls! That hurts more!

JEANNINE:
We phone the rest of the gang to tell them we'll eat somewhere else and we don't tell Madeleine, that's all.

MADELEINE:
They needn't bother cheating on the candles either, 'cause I'll tell the whole world how old she is.

LAURETTE:
But that's an awful thing to do. What if she shows up and there's no one there?

JEANNINE:
You'd rather be there?

LAURETTE:
Of course not, but couldn't you just phone her and tell her the party's cancelled . . .

JEANNINE:
Me, phone her? I never want to talk to her again, I'm too ashamed!

MADELEINE:
And if the others don't know she wears a wig, now they're gonna know!

JEANNINE:

>Look, relax! We'll have the party somewhere else and that's that. We'll straighten it out with Madeleine some other time, but not today. I'll phone the girls back and tell them we're going to the Laurier. You run over and get the present. But above all, don't do anything else, you hear me?

LAURETTE:

>I'm not a baby!

JEANNINE:

>You're worse than a baby, dear! A baby isn't dangerous! Bye!

>*She hangs up.*

LAURETTE:

>This is awful!

MADELEINE:

>I'll grind her wig into the cake! I'll leave her there with her silk stocking on her head and I'll mail the wig to Gaston, special delivery!

LAURETTE:

>Poor Madeleine! We can't treat her like that!

MADELEINE:

>They don't realize it, but they've done me a favour, the fools!

LAURETTE:

>I'm gonna phone her and tell her not to go.

>*She dials MADELEINE's number.*

MADELEINE:

>I'd decided not to get my revenge . . . But now, I CAN'T RESIST!

MADELEINE's phone rings.

If that's them trying to apologize, they'll just have to wait. This is the chance of a lifetime! My fangs are growing long! My nails are getting sharp!

JEANNINE:
> It'd be just like Laurette to phone Madeleine and tell her everything. It's not a heart she's got, it's a big lump of melted candy!

JEANNINE dials LAURETTE's number.

LAURETTE:
> Why doesn't she answer?

MADELEINE:
> I can see it now . . . I come into the restaurant. They're all there, having their party for that stinking corpse, Madeleine Simard! I hide behind a flower pot like a panther.

JEANNINE:
> I was right, she's on the phone! Bloody hell!

LAURETTE:
> Answer it! Answer it!

MADELEINE:
> That telephone's driving me nuts!

> *She takes the phone off the hook and places the receiver on the table.*

> *LAURETTE can hear everything she says.*

> I leap out at their table so fast they don't know what hit them. "Surprise!" And then . . .

LAURETTE:
> What? Hello?

MADELEINE:

Down we go, Madeleine's head right in the cake!
Her ugly puss all covered with cream!

JEANNINE:

I'll phone Madeleine just to be sure. But if she answers,
I'm hanging up!

MADELEINE:

Then I pull off her wig, whack her across the face
with it two or three times and smear it around in the
other's plates!

LAURETTE:

Dear God, Madeleine, don't do that! Hello? Hello?

JEANNINE:

That's exactly what I thought.

She hangs up.

That does it, I've had it! I'm not changing the party,
I'm not doing anything! And I'm not going! I wash
my hands of it!

MADELEINE:

What else could I do to her? What? I'll slap her face!
That's it, some nice big slaps across the face! POW!
POW! POW!

The lights start to fade.

LAURETTE:

Madeleine! Madeleine! Have you gone out of your
mind? Answer me, Madeleine!

MADELEINE:

Maybe I'll take some Javex and wash out her
mouth . . .

JEANNINE:
>I'll try her one last time . . .

LAURETTE:
>Madeleine!

MADELEINE: *getting crazier all the time*
>Or a shotgun!

LAURETTE:
>Madeleine!

MADELEINE:
>Or maybe a butcher knife!

JEANNINE:
>Damn her!

>*She hangs up.*

>Oh to hell with them all!

LAURETTE:
>Madeleine!

MADELEINE:
>That's it, a butcher knife, and I'll mix their blood around in buckets full of Bar B-Q sauce!

>*Blackout.*